Hi Dolores, hope This helps you

PUTT

LIKE

THE

PROS

Happy Birthday!

Dad &
Betty

PUTT LIKE THE PROS

**Dave Pelz's Scientific
Way to Improving Your
Stroke, Reading
Greens, and Lowering
Your Score**

DAVE PELZ with NICK MASTRONI

 HarperPerennial

A Division of HarperCollinsPublishers

First HarperPerennial edition published 1991.

Designer: Laura Hough
Illustrations by Katherine Lynn Pelz

Library of Congress Cataloging-in-Publication Data

Pelz, Dave.
  Putt like the pros.

  1. Putting (Golf)   I. Mastroni, Nick.   II. Title.
GV979.P8P45   1989   796.352′35   86-46095
ISBN 0-06-015745-3

ISBN 0-06-092078-5 (pbk.)
        94 95 RRD 10 9

DEDICATION

To Lil and Ed, the greatest golfers I've ever known. You were playing three times a week when you taught me to play over 40 years ago, and you still play three times a week today. Good golfing and I love you.

ACKNOWLEDGMENT

I would like to acknowledge the encouragement and patience of my family, Laura, Kathy, Little D and Helen Kay, without which my lifestyle in golf, and this book, would not exist. I also want to thank all the PGA Tour professionals who have allowed me to share in their knowledge and experiences. And in particular I appreciate the feedback and concern of my favorite Tour professionals in the world, Tom Jenkins, Allen Miller, Jim Simons and D.A. Weibring. Without their sincere and relentless involvement and sharing of what does and doesn't work, I would never have learned anything significant about this incredible game.

Contents

Contents

PART III: Feel and Touch in Putting

PART IV: The Implements of Putting

PART V: The Mental Side of Putting

Introduction: With Jack Nicklaus—In the Beginning

My position in the game of golf may be unique. I am not a licensed PGA professional, yet I have the pleasure of teaching and working with both PGA Tour professionals and amateur golfers from around the world. I research and develop new golf products and golfing techniques. I write technical articles for golf magazines and I conduct schools on the short game. I started out specializing in putting and now have developed interests in all aspects of the game—but especially in the shots played within 100 yards of the green. A little unusual, I guess, for a guy whose career as a scientist in the space program for NASA seemed firmly entrenched!

If I can pinpoint one thing that served as the catalyst for my early motivation to learn all I could about the science of putting, it is this: I am a contemporary of the greatest golfer in history, Jack Nicklaus. Not only did I grow up in golf during the same years that Nicklaus did, but I competed directly against him.

I could not beat Nicklaus. Ever. At the time (and for quite a while afterward) this failure was extremely frustrating to me. Thankfully I am no longer traumatized and with good reason; Jack Nicklaus has been confounding the best players in the world for over a quarter of a century now. What I enjoy saying, when I am asked about Jack's ability, is, "Naw, he's not really that good; he's just been on a thirty-year hot streak!"

Let me begin at the college level and work my way through the web of events that brought me to where I am and why I can help your putting game.

A RUDE COMEUPPANCE

As a young man, I always dreamed of competing on the PGA Tour and following in the footsteps of the likes of Byron Nelson and Arnold Palmer. I worked hard on my game all through high school and managed to earn a golf scholarship to Indiana University. While at Indiana, I majored in physics and minored in mathematics and philosophy. At the time, though, mastering my studies rated a distant second to my goal of becoming a great player. I went to Indiana to learn to play golf well enough to do it for a living; physics, math, and philosophy were just some fun I had along the way.

I worked very hard on my golf in my first couple of years, with moderate success. However, as I competed in the Big Ten Conference I came into more and more frequent contact with a fellow who played on the Ohio State golf team, named Jack Nicklaus.

One thing this fellow Nicklaus could do even back then was beat everybody in sight, including yours truly. During my career at Indiana, I played in competition against Jack on a total of twenty-two occasions, be it in individual matches, tri-matches held among three schools, or stroke-play tournaments. And dishearteningly for me, while I played well on several occasions in these direct competitions, the scoreboard read: Jack Nicklaus 22, Dave Pelz 0.

Along about the end of my junior year I decided to have a meeting with my good friend, Bob Fitch, the Indiana golf coach. I asked him, "Why in the world can't I beat this guy

Nicklaus?" I was a reasonably good ball striker. On several of the occasions when I had lost to Jack I had played as well as or better than he from tee to green. With regard to my putting, I had taken lessons from a number of professionals. All of them told me I had a good, solid stroke and that if I had any problems with putting, they were all in my head. So I asked my coach, "What's wrong with me? Don't I have the heart, the guts, the courage it takes to be a winner?"

My coach was very encouraging. He told me that I certainly didn't lack the talent or the ability to bear down and "grind" when it counted. He did point out, though, that I was competing against Nicklaus at a tremendous disadvantage because I was not as well prepared to play golf as Nicklaus was. He reminded me that Nicklaus never had to work during the summer. Jack hit thousands and thousands of practice balls, worked on his putting incessantly, and he competed in tournaments every week. On the other hand, I was trying to earn money during the summers as well as improve my game. (One summer I had worked a full-time night job in an engine-testing laboratory while attempting to play golf during the day.)

My coach believed I was not well enough prepared for top-level competition. In particular, he emphasized my need to putt and putt and putt, to get my stroke so "grooved" that my confidence would soar. He convinced me that more time and effort on the greens would do the trick.

I certainly took this advice to heart. In fact, I obtained permission from the dean of the Indiana University Science Department to carry an unusual course load. In the fall (non-golf) semester I took an extra-heavy load of twenty-two credit hours. This allowed me to take just nine credit hours in the spring semester, so that I finished my classes by 10:30 every morning and was at the golf course before 11:00 a.m. every day.

I hit tons of practice balls that semester but, more to the point, I practiced my putting for *four hours* a day, rain or shine, because putting was the weakness with which I was most concerned. This regimen was typical of me in that I went a little overboard, but I had committed myself to being the "best-prepared" golfer on the planet.

How much do you think this concentrated practice did for my game? That year, my stroke average went *up* by one-tenth of a stroke! I had become a slightly worse player. In the Big Ten Championship which was played on Indiana University's home course, Jack Nicklaus (who else?) won while I finished way back in the pack. It was a terrible disappointment.

FROM THE SPACE RACE TO GOLF RESEARCH

With school finished, I realized there was no way I could compete with the Tour pros. And I thank my lucky stars for that decision. I couldn't even beat Jack Nicklaus, an overweight college kid! I knew he was good, but I never guessed that he would become the foremost player in history—that he was the toughest golfer in the world against whom to judge myself. I could have been much better than I actually was and still not have been good enough to make it on the Tour. Jack was exactly what I needed to force me toward the right choice, to give up my golf-playing plans.

Instead, I took a job in physics, working at the Goddard Space Flight Center, outside of Washington, D.C. I spent nearly fifteen years there, doing research on the upper atmospheres of the earth and other planets in our solar system. I was involved in the "golden age" of the space race.

Eventually I became a senior scientist, with responsibilities for several international satellite programs. With that post came significant worldwide travel and the opportunity to associate with tremendous people, the best minds science had to offer. I loved my work and I was also happily married and raising three wonderful children.

Along with this very fine position and the challenges it offered, I continued my love affair with the game of golf. I guess it still nagged me that I had not been good enough to play the Tour. And one day it struck me that my situation offered a great opportunity to improve my game—not through incessant, mindless practice, but through the application of science. Why couldn't I use this scientific expertise and technology to do research on my own putting—research that had never been done before?

I must admit that I am a stubborn individual. It still bothered me that I never beat Jack Nicklaus. I had played football, basketball, tennis, Ping-Pong, and other sports alongside the guy, and at the time I felt I could beat him at any sport besides golf. So why did he always beat me like a drum on the golf course? Was it his mind that was better? Based on our academic credentials, I didn't believe that was the case. Did he work harder, care more about the game than I did? No one worked harder or cared more than I did. Was it his hand-eye coordination, his athletic ability that were superior? I had received a scholarship to play college basketball as well as golf. I didn't believe he was a better athlete.

After soul-searching for over a decade, the only answer I came up with was that Jack Nicklaus could putt so much better than I could that it wasn't funny. He was a great lag putter, he almost never three-putted, and he seemed to make every one of those 4- to 6-foot "testers." I thought, if he can do it, maybe I can learn!

So in 1970 I began measuring what happens when the putterhead hits the ball. What does the ball do? How do I move my hands? Do I rotate, break, or cock my wrists? How consistent are my movements? When do they happen? And so on, seemingly to infinity!

At this point I had no intention of turning pro, but I still wanted to become as good a player as I could. I had remained a good amateur player, a scratch golfer who won his "home club" championship frequently. But I found that when I went to a national event such as the U.S. Amateur or U.S. Open qualifiers, I never quite made the grade.

However, in 1974, as a result of my putting research and

the changes I made because of them, I played my best golf ever. I shot 68 in tournaments at least a half-dozen times that summer and I was rarely over par. I finally qualified for and played in the U.S. Amateur Championship, and I was medalist in the Maryland State Amateur Championship. Friends kidded me, asking if I had quit my job and was playing golf all week long. That is how evident the improvement was! The truth of the matter was simply that my putting had improved vastly. My 1974 experience convinced me forever that putting is a learned rather than a God-given talent.

INTO THE GOLF BUSINESS

During this research from 1970 to 1974, I developed what is now called the Teacher Putter, a training device I'll talk about in later chapters. And, perhaps because of the exposure I was getting with my improved play, a group of business people approached me with the idea of starting a company to manufacture and sell Teacher Putters. In the fall of 1974 that is what I did, while still working for NASA at the Goddard Space Flight Center.

I quickly realized the headaches with and involvement of starting a new company, and the enterprise was affecting my work at NASA. I discussed the problem with the man I respected most—my division chief at NASA—and he suggested I take an educational leave of absence for one year. I could learn the golf business, learn about business in general, and then return to my work at NASA as an improved employee with no risk or loss of security. For a man with a wife and three children, it was a wonderful opportunity.

I took the plunge in January of 1975. It was the humblest of beginnings in the basement of my home. I immediately fell in love with the golf business, but almost as quickly I proceeded to lose almost everything I had. In that first year, I lost all my investors' money while I obtained a solid year's research on the game of golf. I loved thinking about the game and researching it and talking about it; the only thing I didn't like was losing money! But always an optimist, I somehow didn't foresee the financial difficulties that lay ahead.

At the end of 1975 I officially resigned from NASA, mortgaging my home and two cars to fund the business. And in 1976, I lost all that money! Some people said I designed good golf equipment, but no one ever accused me of being a good businessman!

Still, I believed I had a better way of doing things, that I could build better golf products and eventually succeed. In the next couple of years, things started to improve—meaning that I wasn't losing money nearly as fast!

It became a policy of mine to introduce at least one new product every year. In 1979 I brought out the Teacher Alignment Computer, described in detail in Chapter 8. This device turned out to be a popular product, and it helped my company become profitable for the first time. Naturally I was ecstatic.

By 1980, I had formed a partnership with a manufacturing firm to produce full sets of clubs. For a time, the manufacturing process took place in Chicago, while I remained in the Washington, D.C. area. This arrangement proved unwieldy; it became clear that the entire operation should be based in a warm-weather climate, so I could simultaneously be involved with production and do the necessary outdoor research.

In 1982 I moved with the entire manufacturing operation to Texas and introduced Dave Pelz Featherlite golf clubs. In 1986 I left the manufacturing business completely, convinced that my niche in golf was in the area of research, development, and education. Today my company, Independent Golf Research, is based in Austin, Texas, and we are doing just that. We perform independent research and testing for various companies and associations in the golf industry, develop products under contract, teach golf schools, and write technical articles and opinions for golf publications. I eat, drink, talk, and sleep golf every day, and I love it. I have hardly taken a day's vacation since I got into golf over ten years ago. But when I do take one, I go play golf!

Enough of my own story. I have detailed my personal background in the hope that you will see how much golf means to me and from what direction this book is coming. I am a golf nut now and have been so for over forty years. For the last eighteen, I have studied the game from a scientific point of view. That is where this book is coming from: the halls of the Indiana University Physics Department, the laboratories of the Goddard Space Flight Center, the putting greens of the PGA Tour, and the frustrations of a formerly bad putter.

This book brings you knowledge and understanding in five major areas. In Part I, The Research on Putting, you will learn about the outside influences which affect every putt you stroke—influences you may never have even thought about. What you learn here will lead you to Part II, The Mechanics of Putting—the techniques and exercise drills that will vastly improve your stroke. Part III, Feel and Touch in Putting, will show you how to develop the touch for distance to a degree you never imagined possible. In Part IV, The Implements of Putting, I will discuss various aspects of putters themselves. And finally, in Part V, The Mental Side of Putting, I show you what you need to know to help you through those periods when your confidence is gone, the hole looks like a pinhole, and you are thinking of finally taking up tennis.

Once you begin to understand that putting is a science and you start to learn about that science, you have made the first big step toward becoming a better putter—and a better golfer. So, let's proceed!

PART I: The Research on Putting

1 How Important Is Putting?

During my first four years working full time in golf, from 1975 through 1978, I measured the performance of golfers over many hundreds of rounds of golf. These were rounds played by both PGA and LPGA Tour professionals, by good amateurs and by average players as well.

Figure 1.1 provides a complete breakdown of the percentages of shots by category that golfers played in the rounds charted. As you can see, putting represents *43 percent* of all shots played. All your iron shots combined equal only about one-third the number of strokes with the putter. (That should really make you think about where to devote your practice time. Most golfers practice iron shots more than anything else.)

What is a "putt"? I define a putt as any stroke made with the putter in which the player uses a normal putting stroke, including strokes made when the ball is putted from the fringe. I do not include any trouble shots that might be hit with a putter, such as banging the ball up a steep bank or hitting a putter left-handed (for righties) to knock the ball away from a tree trunk. Real, honest-to-goodness putting strokes only!

Based on this definition, the 43 percent value of putting

3

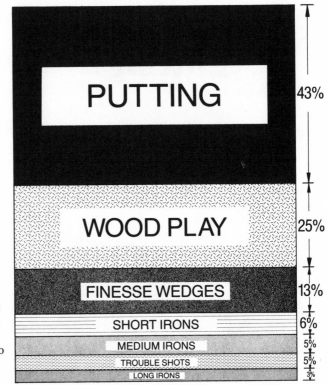

FIGURE 1.1: Putting is 43 percent of the game of golf. An improvement in your putting is the surest way to lower your score.

holds up very well for all golfers except those who score over 100. The professional who shoots 70 will average about thirty strokes with the putter; most 85 shooters will use the putter around thirty-five times; and the 95 shooter will putt about thirty-eight times per round.

In reality, putting is *more than half* the game! Why? First, the putt is the "terminal" shot on every hole (except, of course, if you should hole out from off the green, and that occurs only rarely). If you happen to hit your drive, fairway iron, or chip shot poorly, you can still recover and save your par. In fact, often it is still possible to make a birdie while making one bad swing on a hole. But when you miss a putt, you have lost a stroke you can never get back. You simply add one stroke to your score, then you putt again!

Second, putting is the part of the game that comes under

the closest scrutiny. The rest of your foursome is standing close by, watching. Without a doubt it is the most pressure-filled aspect of golf. Third, I am convinced that if you have developed an accurate, reliable putting stroke, you automatically hold a tremendous advantage over less-talented putters, even in the *long game!* On iron shots, you don't have to gamble on knocking your approach shot stiff to a tightly tucked pin. If you hit the middle of the green, you know you will get a sure two-putt and you might sink your first putt anyway. Confidence in your putting can take a lot of pressure off your tee shots as well. You can play your drive to the safest area rather than risk trouble by trying to get into "Position A" for that perfect approach shot.

The end result is that if you are confident in your putting and that confidence is based on a technically sound, repeatable stroke, you will take pressure off your full swing—which means you will execute better in the long game, too. You can, in effect, build your entire game around the soundness of your putting. It is amazing how free and easy your swing can become when you believe that, even if you make a mistake, you can save yourself with the putter.

So now you see why I say that, although statistically putting represents 43 percent of the game, in reality it is more than 50 percent. Your putting ability has a profound effect on how you play *all* your shots, how you score, and how much enjoyment you get from this great game.

2 Putting Is a Science, Not a Black Art

Most golf instructors view the well-executed full golf swing as a mechanical masterpiece, the compilation of many body motions into a rhythmic sequence that sends the ball into near-earth space in a well-planned, predictable flight trajectory. You can "assemble" a golf swing. You can learn it. Your club professional can teach it to you. No, you will probably never hit the ball with the power and precision of a Jack Nicklaus or a Tom Kite, but you can see definite improvement over time if you work on your swing under a professional's guidance.

By comparison, putting is considered a "black art." I have devoted myself to golf and particularly to the area of putting for the past fourteen years, and the notion I have lived with during that time is: putting is a God-given talent; you are either born with it or you are not. Most golfers believe this. And the superficial evidence most golfers see validates this belief for them. They may practice on the putting green diligently for a while, but they get no better. So they say to themselves, "I was born a lousy putter and I guess I'm going to stay that way."

Even among the club professionals who teach the game,

6

it is a widely held notion that putting is a black art. In the last decade I have spoken at seminars to more than 4,000 club professionals. Most of these pros teach the full swing, yet I have found only a few who teach putting. There are no commonly accepted rules, procedures, or methods to follow in teaching or learning putting, and no one talks about learning to be a great putter.

LEARNING TO LEARN

The putting stroke is certainly not difficult to execute. Mechanically, it is the simplest motion in golf. There is no need to move your head, your knees, or your hips. You only need a few of the hundreds of muscles that are involved in the full swing. If anything, you would think that golfers would expect their putting strokes to hold up much better than their full swings do.

I believe that putting is actually an easy act to perform. My own putting stroke has become so simple that it's almost a joke. It took me thirty years to understand how to learn to putt better, then just six months to actually putt better!

You cannot—I repeat, cannot—learn the proper mechanics for the execution of the putting stroke simply by going out and practicing with monklike dedication on a putting green. Yes, you can sharpen your touch for distance that way. But improve the mechanics of your stroke on the practice green? Not likely! How can you improve your stroke mechanics when you don't know what is wrong with them?

Most players who ask me for putting lessons both want and expect me to provide some "mechanical" tips: try a certain type of stance, employ a unique putting grip, stand tall to the ball or crouch, and so on. Many of you who read this book are expecting this, too. So I might as well tell you right now that, while I will address these areas which many consider the very basis of teaching putting, I consider them only secondary factors in the creation of a solid putting stroke. And I won't get around to discussing these secondary putting factors until Chapter 11.

YOUR FEEDBACK IS FOOLING YOU

The fundamental problem in the quest to become an excellent putter is the fact that you rarely get accurate feedback on the quality of your putting stroke when you practice it. For that matter, you rarely get useful feedback on the golf course, either. It is very, very difficult to differentiate between a perfectly executed stroke and an imperfect one. I am certain that if you have played golf for any significant amount of time, you have executed many perfect putting strokes. The problem is that you never know when you have made a perfect stroke or when you have made a bad one.

Why have you executed perfect strokes while not knowing it? Because the result of that perfect stroke may have been a putt which never even went *near* the hole! (As you'll see later, there are numerous reasons why a perfectly struck putt may miss.) You had no way of knowing what caused the miss; you received no accurate *feedback*, so you assumed that you pulled or pushed the putt. As a result, you probably changed something in your very next stroke!

It is amazing how many golfers who have put a great deal of time, effort, and caring into the game cannot realize how inaccurate feedback blinds them to the realities of their putting. I will never forget the classic argument a golfer presented during one of my seminars. He stood up and said, "Putting is the best part of my game. I can really putt." I asked him what evidence he had to prove it. He replied, "Last week, I sank a really tough downhill, sidehill twenty-footer at the seventeenth hole. Then on the eighteenth, I had a monstrous uphill forty-five–footer and knocked that one in too! After the round, I was watching a tournament in the

8

lounge on TV, and I saw Jack Nicklaus miss from six, ten, and five feet on the last three holes."

This guy thought he was a better putter than Jack Nicklaus! I submit, however, that this opinion wasn't very accurate. I was curious about this fellow's stroke so I tested him and, sure enough, I found that his stroke was none too good. But by chance the day before, he had pulled his putter across the line just the right amount, opened the blade through impact a little bit, and misread the putt so that it hit a spike mark in the green which twisted the ball just the right amount and he sank a 20-footer and a 45-footer. And he thought this made him a great putter! Well, I can guarantee you that Nicklaus would clean this man's clock 99 times out of 100, if they putted enough holes for statistics to be meaningful.

WHY DO WE "LOSE IT"?

There is another point to consider about putting that is unique among all movements in sports. In almost any sport that involves hand-eye coordination and/or other physical abilities, the more you practice (while obtaining reasonably competent coaching), the better you will perform. This is true in passing or catching a football, shooting a basketball, serving a tennis ball, and pitching or hitting a baseball.

However, if you went on the PGA Tour and asked all the stars, "At what time in your life did you putt your best?" they would say they putted best somewhere between the ages of fourteen and seventeen. Now I am talking about the best players in the world, the ones you watch on TV. It is true of the great Jack Nicklaus. He putted a great deal better as a teenager than he does today. Johnny Miller believes he was the best putter there ever was when he was about sixteen years old. Almost all the pros say things to this effect.

Putting seems to be a gift bestowed on the young and

9

innocent, but is gradually but inexorably spirited away as players age and become more sophisticated and talented in other aspects of the game. However, I don't agree with the notion that as players get older, they *must* putt worse. What I believe really happens is that the longer they practice while receiving inaccurate feedback, the more mediocre they indeed become. And I have a specific example from my own experience that supports this theory.

While working at Goddard Space Flight Center in the late '60s and early '70s, I played at a club which had quite a few junior golfers but didn't have a strong teaching program for them. I thought perhaps I could help these kids. After all, I was a scratch player and I thought I knew what I was doing. So I became coach of the club's junior team, and I watched these youngsters develop their games over a period of years. I saw something that was both surprising and perplexing.

We have all seen kids twelve to sixteen years old who can putt the eyes out of the hole. It seems like everything they hit from inside 10 feet is "automatic," and they hole an amazing percentage of long ones as well. I noticed that the more these kids practiced, the more mediocre they became. Great putters at age fourteen became average putters four years later.

On the other side of the coin, there were golfers of the same age who did not yet have a feel for the putting game. They were really terrible putters. But by practicing hard for a couple of years, they improved to where they, too, could be considered "average."

In other words, I learned from these juniors that if you practice hard on a putting green, you will not necessarily become better; if you're a good putter to start with, you will become more *average!* This is exactly what happened to me when I followed that exhaustive putting practice regimen during my years at Indiana University. It is what happens over the long haul, even to some very talented Tour pros. And, it may be happening to you, too.

POOR PRACTICE PRODUCES POOR RESULTS

Practicing on a putting green simply tends to level out all golfers' abilities. That is why out of some 18 million golfers in the United States today, there are only a few who could be called truly great putters. There are thousands of good ones, millions of average ones, and hundreds of thousands of poor ones, too.

When you receive confusing feedback from the green, you compensate for it in your stroke. The human brain is too intelligent to continue missing putt after putt in the same way. But as you move from one spot on the putting green to another, the feedback changes and thus your own compensations change, too. That is why you never seem to develop a consistent stroke!

BE A "PHILOSOPHER" ON THE GREENS

Failing to make "easy" putts should make philosophers of us all. What should we learn? First off, we have to understand that a golfer can't sink every putt. Only if you are willing to learn to execute the most mechanically sound and consistent putting stroke possible will you become better and sink more putts. And in order to putt well you have to understand what "good putting" really is.

3 How Well Can Man or Machine Putt?

Why do almost all golfers complain about their putting? Are there reasons why golfers never live up to their putting expectations? Why don't they get their expected accuracy? I decided to find out.

My first experiment was to see how many putts could conceivably be made from various distances by a "perfect" putter. In an attempt to find out, I built a putting machine I thought would strike the ball perfectly. This was a tripod device with a bearing from which a regular putter was suspended at the normal angle. A motorized mechanism pulled the clubhead back from the ball a specific distance and then released it into the downstroke.

I took this machine to the putting green. I set it up on the correct line for each putt and tested it on putts of various distances. What I found was that I missed a lot of putts no matter how I adjusted the aim. Naturally I was disconcerted.

During this testing, a fellow walked out, introduced himself as Bert Yancey, and asked me what I was doing. Bert Yancey at that time was one of the top PGA Tour players in the world. And, interestingly, Bert was widely acclaimed as being the very best putter. In fact, he held the record for the fewest putts (102) in a 72-hole tournament. (He won the tournament, so you know he wasn't just playing poorly, missing greens, chipping close, and tapping in "gimmes.")

I told Bert I was doing some research on putting, and he said, "If you're taking data with that machine, I don't think it's going to be very accurate, because I can putt better than it can." Both being very competitive people, we immediately started a contest and, sure enough, Bert beat the machine! Rather chagrined, I took my invention home and found the problems that were causing deviation in the strokes. During my redesign, I discovered I needed a totally different method of ball propulsion to provide the accuracy of roll necessary to measure how many putts it is possible to make from a given distance—and to have a chance of beating Bert Yancey!

Thus began work on an apparatus that I now consider the world's best putter, called the True Roller.

HOW THE TRUE ROLLER WORKS

The True Roller (Figure 3.1) consists of an 8-foot-long ramp made of two circular, precision-machined rods spaced exactly 1 inch apart. There is a release mechanism which holds a golf ball the way your thumb and forefinger would. An adjustment knob allows you to move the release mechanism up or down the ramp as much as needed. Thus you can start the ball from the correct height on the ramp so that it will gather exactly the right amount of speed to roll the appropriate distance to the hole. The release mechanism can be moved up or down in increments of one-thousandth of an inch (about one-third the width of a strand of human hair.)

You "putt" the ball by pushing a button that moves the release-mechanism fingers out from the sides of the ball (see Figure 3.1). After it is released, the ball starts rolling down the ramp pulled only by the force of gravity. The ball carries exactly the same amount of energy every time because gravity is the most constant force on earth. When the ball rolls

13

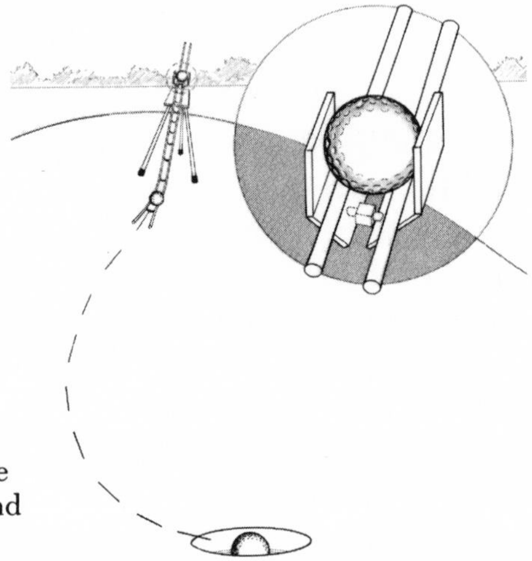

FIGURE 3.1: The True Roller, when aimed properly, starts the ball on a perfect line, speed, and roll every time.

down the ramp, there is absolutely no bounce, no spin, nothing to divert the ball. It is just a pure, true roll. Where the ramp is close to the green, it curves onto the green's surface and the rails are gradually spread apart. So the golf ball, which has a diameter of 1.68 inches, rolls progressively lower between the rails, then glides gently onto the putting surface with no bounce whatsoever.

Another feature of the True Roller is the control device by which the aim is adjusted, in increments of one-thousandth of an inch. Of course, this adjustment capability represents extreme aiming accuracy. No human being could possibly aim his or her own putter that well. But I felt I needed this advantage to have a chance to beat Bert Yancey (who had become a good friend as a result of our involvement with putting and putters).

SOMETHING WAS STILL MISSING

Once I finished building the True Roller, I took it to a putting green, making certain the green was in excellent condition. I set it up and adjusted it for the optimum line and speed, then started rolling putts with it. Now remember that I could repeat the speed with which I rolled the ball every time. I could repeat the aim of the putt every time as well, and I could adjust either of these factors to tolerances far closer than any human being could. I believed I had achieved the ultimate accuracy. Once I put a ball between the "fingers" of the True Roller and released it, the ball had to go in the hole every time. Right?

Wrong. To my complete consternation, I found that the True Roller was still missing lots of putts! What was the problem? I tried to make a scientific determination at this point. Were the missed putts caused by inconsistencies in the True Roller itself? Was the surface of the green changing, making some putts miss while others rolled into the center of the cup? Was there a problem of differences among golf balls? Or was the hole moving?

I quickly eliminated this last possibility. However, I knew the True Roller itself or the putting surface could still be at fault. To check both of these factors I arranged to use a brand-new, high-quality, slate-bed pool table to roll the balls on, after ascertaining that the surface of the table was truly flat. I made all the necessary adjustments in the True Roller so as to roll the balls into the center of the far corner pocket, and the balls were to roll at the perfect speed as well. The surface of the pool table was faster than most real greens, but as long as the surface provided a true line of roll and the speed stayed constant, conditions were what I needed for my test.

I tested thousands of putts on that pool table, and putt after putt after putt rolled into the far pocket. The fact that they were rolling into the pocket really wasn't good enough, though, because not all the putts were rolling into the *center* of the pocket. On some putts there was a variance of 1 inch or more to either side. Now, the ball was rolling a distance of only about 8 feet. If the putt were longer, the error could be enough to make it miss the hole, even with perfect alignment and a perfect roll on the putt.

At this point, I took many additional measurements that proved the True Roller was doing its job. It accurately aimed and rolled the balls. So my next efforts were directed to measuring those little round white balls.

4 The Golf Ball Can Fool You

When I began looking carefully at golf balls, I found three major areas of concern regarding their "puttability." First, some golf balls are not perfectly spherical, or round. Second, even those balls that are spherical may not be balanced properly. And third, the construction technique and material of the ball can make a difference! I did some testing in each of these three areas to determine the effect, if any, on the way putts roll.

EGGS AND FOOTBALLS DON'T ROLL STRAIGHT

It is obvious that all not-perfectly round balls cannot roll straight and true along an intended line, even if they are started correctly. It was easy to determine if a ball was perfectly round by using precision machined rings and pins, which have an inside diameter just larger than the ball's 1.68 inches. A ball that is perfectly round should fit and turn through this apparatus without interference. While most of the not-perfectly round balls are "caught" in quality control tests by the manufacturers, I still found a few. So I elimi-

16

nated all remaining not-perfectly round balls from my subsequent testing.

BALANCE: THE UNSEEN FACTOR

Since all the remaining balls were perfectly round, could any of them be out of balance? If so, would this make a difference in the way they rolled? This problem was more complex.

To determine if a ball was out of balance I put it in a solution, spinning it and observing the consistency of its rotation as it slowed down and came to a stop (see Figure 4.1, page 20). Based on each ball's particular behavior, I could determine whether a ball was perfectly balanced, slightly out of balance, or badly out of balance.

Bear in mind that I did this research several years ago, so it may not reflect accurately the condition of balls you might purchase today. Still, my tests showed startlingly that no more than one ball out of two dozen is perfectly balanced! And some brands tested much worse for balance than others.

Now don't get irate with golf-ball manufacturers. Believe me, it is extremely difficult to make a perfect golf ball! Manufacturers spend millions of dollars researching and constructing golf balls, and they do an excellent job. A lot of things in this world aren't perfect, and golf balls are just one of them.

In order to find out if an out-of-balance ball could roll imperfectly to the degree that it would cause a perfectly stroked putt to miss the hole, I separated the balls into categories of perfect, slightly out-of-balance, and badly out-of-balance. (The slightly out-of-balance category was by far the largest.) I then rolled the balls down the True Roller, across the pool table again, knowing which balls were which. Sure enough, the perfectly balanced balls consistently rolled into the center of the corner pocket.

I placed the imperfect balls in the True Roller with what I had determined was their "lighter" side on the left. I found that as these balls rolled out of the True Roller and onto the table, they consistently turned toward the right (toward the heavy side). If I reversed the ball in the True Roller, the ball then moved consistently to the left. When the lighter side was placed on the top or bottom of the True Roller, the ball rolled heavy side over light side—right along the intended line!

As I mentioned earlier, none of these balls (with the exception of a couple of badly misbalanced ones) turned so much as to miss the pocket, but they all turned consistently toward the heavy side. So there is no doubt: the ball itself *must* be considered a factor that can influence the roll of a putt.

How Do Your Golf Balls Rate in the Balance Test?

Should you want to test your golf balls for balance, here's how to do it. I suggest you try it on one or two dozen balls of each brand you use, so you can see for yourself the measurable differences from one ball to the next and from one manufacturer to another.

Fill a glass tumbler or a cup with hot tap water until several inches deep. For every inch of water, add one to two tablespoons Epsom salts. Add salts until a test ball floats, with the top of the ball just above the water line. Next add just one drop of Jet-Dri dishwasher despotting agent to reduce the surface tension, or friction, of the water; the balls will then spin more freely in the solution.

Test one ball at a time. Don't just drop the ball in; spin it in the solution by turning it between your thumb and forefinger. The ball will rotate for many seconds, gradually slowing down. Notice *how* the ball comes to a stop (see Figure 4.1). If it comes to a gradual stop without any rocking motion, put a dot on top with a felt-tip permanent-ink pen. Remove the ball

(continued)

and spin it again. If it again comes to a halt without rocking and stops with a *different* area on top, you have a ball with no measurable heavy or light side. (If it had one, the heavy side would always settle at the bottom.) Remove the ball, dry it off, and put a second dot next to the first. The two dots signify a perfectly balanced ball. Save these balls for a tournament or a big match. They will give you some extra confidence for your crucial putts.

Most of the balls you test will slow down, then rock back and forth before coming to a stop. This rocking motion occurs when the ball's heavy side is settling toward the bottom of the glass. The part that settles above the surface is the light side; place a single dot at the very top of the light side.

As you test balls, you will get a feeling for the severity of the rocking motion. Keep the balls that don't rock much separate from your "perfect" balls. Play these in your more important rounds. When you mark and replace your ball on the green, place it with the light side up so that heavy and light sides will roll end over end and your putt's line of roll won't be affected.

A ball that rocks back and forth so violently that it bobs below the surface of the water (caused by a large difference in weight between its heavy and light sides) is what I call a "bobber." The pros don't play bobbers, but of course you may be in a different situation. You've paid good money for your balls, and you may not want to be as choosy. However, if you do find some "bobbers," keep them separate and play them only in your most casual rounds. (Bobbers make great birthday gifts for good friends with whom you compete regularly in your weekend games!)

CONSIDER THE CONSTRUCTION

My next concern was to find out what types of golf ball constructions, if any, tended to roll the truest. I tested balls with balata covers and wound construction, as well as Surlyn-cov-

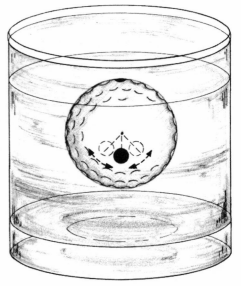

FIGURE 4.1: The Balance Test. A spinning golf ball with off-center weight distribution will slowly come to a stop, with its heaviest side down due to the force of gravity. The light side of the ball will then be above water and can be easily marked (see page 18).

ered balls with both solid and wound interiors. In all, I rolled many thousands of golf balls. I found that for most balata balls rolled by the True Roller, I could control the line of a 10-foot putt to within ¼ to ½ inch, regardless of any heavy or light side position. That is not a tremendous amount of variation. Balata-covered balls are pretty good.

However, the Surlyn balls I tested, whether of solid or wound construction, showed a variance in line of up to 2½ inches to one side or the other, depending on how the ball was placed in the True Roller. This is more than half the width of the cup, which is 4¼ inches in diameter. In other words, I could set up the Surlyn balls so that they would miss the hole to *either* the right or the left, despite starting them on a perfect line with a perfect roll!

This finding surprised me because it seemed reasonable that any imbalances in the balls would be in their inner windings (remember I am not an expert in ball construction). However, the data seem to indicate that the reason for the differences in putting accuracy between Surlyn and balata balls were in the covers themselves (A Surlyn cover is thicker, heavier, and tougher than a balata cover, which is why it doesn't cut when hit poorly.)

Now, *most* of the Surlyn balls tested didn't vary that much; when set in the True Roller so that there were heavy and light sides, on average they would roll off line about 1 inch. However, I consider 1 inch of variance a problem, and if you are already a good putter, so should you! A 1-inch variance in line could really hurt a good putter who is stroking the ball precisely where he or she wants it. On the other hand, a little variation won't matter to a mediocre putter who doesn't roll the ball precisely on line very often. The imbalance might even cause the putt to go in instead of miss!

When I learned that most golf balls have a measurable heavy and light side, of course I informed the Tour pros whom I work with of the details. Many of them began testing and marking their golf balls as a result. So whenever you go to a pro tournament and see a player using a ball with two dots right next to each other, it may indicate a perfectly balanced ball. Usually, the pros keep these balls in a special pocket of their bag and save them for the last few holes of a tournament. This might sound a bit fanatical to you, but I think it is an excellent idea, not only because those balls are going to roll perfectly true, but because the players *know* they are playing with a perfect ball. It gives their confidence a shot in the arm and they are more likely to put their best stroke on it.

ARE YOU A "LONG HITTER" ON THE GREENS?

You know one reason why a ball can roll slightly off line even if you have made a perfect stroke. Did you know that balls of different construction roll different *distances* as well?

What with the profusion of different covers, windings, compressions, and dimple patterns that have come onto the market and the various manufacturers' claims that their balls are the "longest," it occurred to me that these factors might have differing effects on the roll of putts as well. So again I conducted a test.

I used Perfy, the putting robot described in detail in Chapter 10. Perfy actually impacts its putts, whereas with the True Roller no impact contact is made with the ball as it rolls down the ramp. Perfy putted four different types of ball constructions: (1) a 90-compression, balata-covered wound ball; (2) a 90-compression, Surlyn-covered wound ball; (3) a 100-compression, Surlyn-covered wound ball; and (4) a two-piece ball consisting of a Surlyn cover with a solid center (this construction usually doesn't carry a compression rating). These four types of balls account for more than 90 percent of the balls played today.

I set up Perfy to stroke putts a distance of about 30 feet on a green of medium speed. For each test, Perfy hit enough putts so that the results were statistically reliable. The table below shows the average roll of the different types of ball construction.

CENTER CONSTRUCTION	COVER	COMPRESSION	AVERAGE ROLL DISTANCE	DISTANCE DIFFERENTIAL
Wound	Balata	90	29'2"	—
Wound	Surlyn	90	30'4"	+14"
Wound	Surlyn	100	31'9"	+31"
Solid	Surlyn	No Rating	32'0"	+34"

Frankly I expected to see some differences in the length of the roll, but not differences this great. On the green, a switch from a 90-compression balata ball to a Surlyn two-piece ball would give you nearly 3 feet, or 10 percent, more roll on a 30-foot putt!

Between the 90- and 100-compression Surlyn balls, the 100-compression balls rolled farther. On the greens, then, higher compression means greater distance. And the two-piece ball comes off the putterface a trifle faster than the 100-compression Surlyn wound ball.

So when you make a switch from one type of ball to another, be aware that it will result in a difference in your touch on the greens. It is important to remember, too, that on any length of putt, the speed and line factors are always intermingled. A ball that is rolling faster will not break as much as a slower-moving ball, if both start moving along the same line. If you stroke a two-piece Surlyn ball with exactly the same force as a 90-compression balata ball, not only will it roll nearly 10 percent farther, but if the line you are putting on has any degree of break, it will keep a slightly straighter line as well.

I hope now that some of the unexpected rolls you see on the greens will no longer be mysteries. At least you will be aware that ball construction factors *can* affect your putts. Next time you have a day when nothing drops for you, just remember that the ball may have something to do with it. Maybe you will be a little easier on yourself and enjoy yourself more.

With that, let me move on and discuss in the next chapter the factor that, outside of your stroke itself, has the greatest influence on whether or not your putts find the hole: the greens themselves.

5   The Battle of the "Lumpy Doughnut"

Using the True Roller to roll balanced golf balls, I "sank" 1,000 consecutive putts on the pool table mentioned in the previous chapter. The maximum deviation in the line of these putts was less than ¼ inch. Now I knew that both the True Roller and the balls I was using were in fine shape, and I was ready to go back and measure what the real limits were to sinking putts.

THE TRUE ODDS ARE SURPRISING

What percentage of putts do you expect to sink during actual play from a distance of, say, 6 feet from the hole? From 12 feet? Your answers will vary somewhat from the next golfer's, but from posing this question to top golfers of all abilities, I can assure you that most think they should make more putts than are reasonable—for man or machine!

I estimate that most golfers think they should make about 75 percent of all their 6-footers and perhaps 50 percent from 12 feet. As you will see from data provided in this chapter, even if you have developed a very consistent stroke and are putting on an excellent surface, expectations like these

24

are unrealistic. If you make fewer putts than you think you should, eventually you'll start thinking your stroke is at fault. You might decide to totally rebuild it and in the process head down a confusing—and needless—labyrinth of changes, even though many of your "misses" weren't your fault in the first place!

At any rate, it is important that you know just how many putts a "perfect" putter can make, from 3 feet, 6 feet, 12 feet, or anywhere. Data are available for several distances, but let me explain the situation by first concentrating on putts from 12 feet, an important putting distance. Since almost every putt has some degree of break to it, all the putts in the following data included a break of 3 inches (in either direction).

I did this testing at three different golf courses. At each of these courses, I rolled a hundred 12-foot putts on each of the eighteen greens. Between putts the grass along the projected putt line was brushed lightly, so grass "tracking" never occurred. This brushing was done to simulate conditions as they occur on your first try on any putt. The results are shown in Figure 5.1.

Greencastle Country Club, a private club in Silver Springs, Maryland, has relatively low membership fees and a moderate budget for course maintenance. The greens are in good condition, better than at most public courses.

Each bar on the graph represents the percentage of putts sunk on one of the eighteen holes. As you can see, the percentages vary quite a bit from hole to hole, but on the average the True Roller made only *48 percent* of the 1,800 12-foot putts rolled. And remember, this is when each putt was started on the perfect line, with the perfect speed!

Naturally I was very disappointed with the results. I remember watching more than half of these balls miss, and I knew it wasn't the True Roller's fault (do you allow for that possibility when *you* miss)?

Next, I took the True Roller to Bethesda Country Club, in Bethesda, Maryland. This club is much wealthier, commands higher initiation fees and dues, and has a higher main-

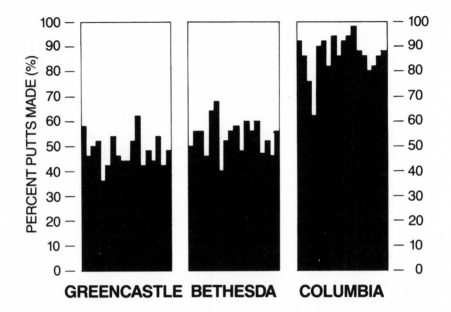

FIGURE 5.1: Different Greens, Different Results. At moderately maintained Greencastle Country Club, the True Roller sank 48 percent from 12
feet; at well-maintained Bethesda Country Club, 54 percent; on the near-
flawless greens of Columbia Country Club, 84 percent. (Individual bars
represent result for each green.)

tenance budget. I was confident that when I ran the same
test on Bethesda's greens, the results would be much better.
However, they were not. After rolling 1,800 12-footers there,
an average of just 54 percent went in!

Finally I arranged for a test at Columbia Country Club
in Chevy Chase, Maryland, a highly respected club that on
one occasion hosted the U.S. Open. The golf professional at
Columbia was a good friend, Bill Strausbaugh, Jr. I explained
to Bill that I wanted to conduct a test on the best-prepared
greens possible to see how many putts could be made. Bill
told me he believed their greens could not be surpassed. He
arranged to have the greens cut on a Monday morning, the
day the course was closed, and made certain that none of
the maintenance crew walked on the greens for the rest of

the day. So I went out on beautiful, untrampled greens, and this time found a big difference in results: 84 percent of these 12-footers went in. The True Roller didn't make all the putts because of wind effects and a few other minor problems; but it was apparent that the lesser amount of play the greens had endured made a tremendous difference in the percentage of putts that the True Roller (or any golfer) can make.

There Are "Can't Miss" Putts and Others You Can't Make

Sometimes the placement of the hole is the reason you miss one putt and make another. Occasionally you will putt on a line whereby the ball must traverse a slight ridge along its path. As the putt moves off the ridge the slightest amount in either direction, it will continue to wander even farther off the line. You may not be able to sink it. This is a "can't make" putt.

Other times the line to the hole runs along a nearly invisible swale. If the ball begins to wander off line, anything it hits tends to funnel it back to the hole. These are the putts you can't miss!

One of the worst mistakes you can make on the practice green is to stroke putt after putt from the same spot if you keep missing, and to refuse to budge until you sink that putt. All you do is convince yourself that your stroke is no good and undermine your confidence. By moving even a few inches, you probably will have a "makeable" putt.

Don't ever "practice" missing in this way! It hurts your mental attitude and is a bad habit to get into.

THE DEADLY EFFECTS OF A DAY'S PLAY

I next wanted to determine how many putts a perfect putter could make on the same green before and after it received heavy play. This time the test green was the huge, beautifully kept practice green at Westchester Country Club, site of the PGA Tour's Manufacturer's Hanover Westchester Classic. I tested 12-footers at dawn on the tournament's pro-am day when the green had just been cut but before golfers had started using it, and the True Roller sank 73 percent. Fine. But at the end of the day, after about 50 pros and 200 amateurs had played the course, the True Roller's "sink" percentage on the identical putt dropped all the way down to 30 percent!

Obviously our putting successes or failures are affected more than we realize by the condition of the putting surface. So let me begin to reveal these living, breathing, growing surfaces to you.

Play Earlier to Sink More

You will make more putts if you play early in the morning rather than in the middle of the afternoon.

No matter what the quality of the greens at the course you play, they will be at their relative best the first thing in the morning, just after they have been mowed. The thousands of footsteps that will be imprinted in their surfaces (along with spike and ball marks) during the day reduce the odds of you getting a true roll as the day progresses.

Explain this benefit to your weekend foursome and see if you can convince them to set their alarm clocks earlier. You'll probably all go home happier at the finish!

WHAT THE GOLF BALL SEES

The grass surface that a golf ball rolls over—and any changes in that surface—can have a tremendous effect on the way the ball rolls. There are numerous types of grass inconsistencies, such as diseases, footprints, ball divots, and spike marks.

Let me talk first about grass diseases. Suppose, for example, there is an area of diseased grass which is shriveled up and lower to the ground than the surrounding healthy grass. If a ball is rolling swiftly, say at the beginning of a 40-foot putt, it will probably run right over the diseased spot without any change in direction. If the ball is rolling slowly or coming to a stop, however, it could be turned to one side or simply bounce, lose energy, and come to a stop more quickly. Both actions significantly change the result of the putt.

The height difference between healthy and diseased grass might seem minuscule to you. But in relation to the golf ball, it's big—up to 10 percent of the ball's 1.68-inch height. And that is significant, just as would be the height of an average roadside curb if you didn't notice it while you were walking. A curb can certainly affect the direction of your walk, and diseased grass can alter a ball's roll!

Although diseases exist on some greens, unrepaired or imperfectly repaired ball divots caused by the impact of shots landing on the green are hazards on every course in the world. Figure 5.2 shows a close-up of what happens when a shot impacts a green, and the mark the ball leaves. Obviously, if your putt rolls over an unrepaired ball divot, it is probably going to be "derailed." When your putt slowly rolls over an unrepaired ball mark it might be equivalent to your tripping over a curb at a street corner and sprawling headlong on your face!

So first you should certainly fix any unrepaired ball marks along your line of putt. And in the name of good sportsmanship and better putting for everyone, *always* fix your

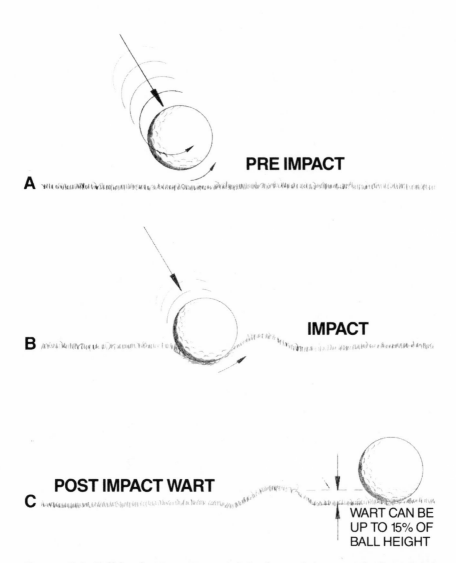

FIGURE 5.2: Ball landing on green with backspin (A) creates ball mark (B), plus a raised wart just past the impact point (C).

own and one other ball mark when you first walk onto the green.

There is another problem, however. Some of the hundreds of previously repaired ball marks that exist on every green are more subtle but still common assailants to the true roll of your putts. Usually a little hump, or wart, remains from the turf that was raised ahead of the ball when it burrowed into the green with backspin. The reason for the wart is that most golfers don't repair their divots correctly. They usually try to smooth the hole made by the ball, but they don't pull back and flatten the raised earth just beyond where the ball hit. The result is that greens are literally covered with these small warts, making it difficult to obtain a true roll across the surface.

The effect of ball marks is usually greater on bent-grass greens than on bermuda. Bent-grass surfaces are usually softer and their root system is much weaker, so the ball's impact digs deeper than on a tougher bermuda-grass surface. (Sometimes you can't even find your divot on bermuda greens.)

Whether you realize it or not, you have probably seen the evidence of warts on your putts many times before. When your rolling putt takes a little hop or bounce, what do you think happened? Did the ball have a "hiccup"? No, it hit a wart. It also cut a little of the distance it would have rolled because it lost energy. And for every time you notice the effect of a wart, there are probably many instances you don't spot. Often the ball hits the side of a wart and is deflected slightly to one side. My slow-motion video replays prove that there are frequent directional changes in putts that the human eye ordinarily does not notice.

FORMATION OF THE "LUMPY DOUGHNUT"

Look at Figure 5.3, an illustration of a footprint on the green. An indentation such as this is caused when a golfer stands still for sixty seconds, as when attending the flagstick for another player. This example is meant to show how greens are living, growing, changing, spongelike surfaces. When you implant a footprint, as with a sponge the indentation will come out with time. However, it takes quite a while for that

31

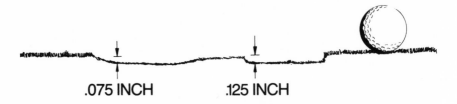

.075 INCH   .125 INCH

FIGURE 5.3: The Footprint may vary in depth of penetration into the green surface; ⅛-inch heel prints are common.

footprint to leave the green entirely. In examining photos of a footprint taken at intervals of several minutes, I found that the deepest part of the heel print was still visible after two and a half hours! It wasn't until the following morning that the footprint was completely gone.

When you play a round of golf, how often are you playing two and a half hours behind the group in front of you? Usually it is more like ten minutes between groups. And your putts are affected by a multitude of footprints, not just one.

Figure 5.4 shows the footprint pattern made on a green by a single foursome. Footprint data were taken from a green just after it had been played by the first group of "dewsweepers," at around 6:30 in the morning. I marked where each golfer hit his ball onto the green and, because of the dew, I was able to map where each player stepped on the green. The first player walked onto the green, marked his ball, replaced it, lined up his putt, addressed the putt, hit it near the hole, repeated his preparations, knocked it in, picked the ball out of the cup, and walked off the green. The other three golfers went through the same procedures; one of the players three-putted and the others two-putted. All in all, this was a fair representation of a foursome's movements on the green.

The end result? This group left more than 500 footprints on the green! As you can see, the footprints are heavily concentrated within a radius of 6 feet from the hole (although almost none are within 1 foot of the hole, since everyone knows it's poor etiquette to step there). The area, with a

The Battle of the "Lumpy Doughnut"

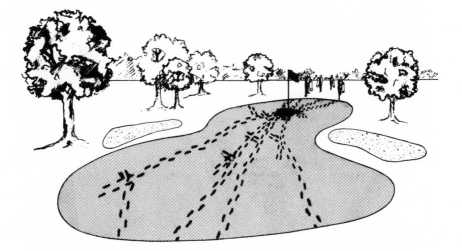

FIGURE 5.4: Traffic Patterns on a Green. In approaching, reading, and executing their putts, the average foursome leaves over 500 footprints on a green. A heavy concentration of these footprints surround the hole.

diameter of about 12 feet, is the embattled zone of golf that I refer to as the "lumpy doughnut" (Figure 5.5). It exists on every practice green and *on every green on every golf course in the world by the end of every playing day.* The greater the amount of play, the more "lumpy" the "lumpy doughnut" is. And, of course, the more footprints there are, the more spike marks there are, too (spike marks are tufts of grass raised by the cleats on golf shoes), which under the rules of golf cannot be repaired. (On the PGA Tour, players refer to these spike marks as "Christmas trees.")

Obviously, conditions within the "lumpy doughnut" are going to cause you to miss some putts. However, the effects of the "lumpy doughnut" are even more drastic than you think. Why? *Because the "lumpy doughnut" exists precisely in the area where your ball is rolling its slowest—when the ball is most susceptible to being knocked off line.* The "lumpy doughnut" is the single most effective reason why golfers never make the percentage of putts they expect to make.

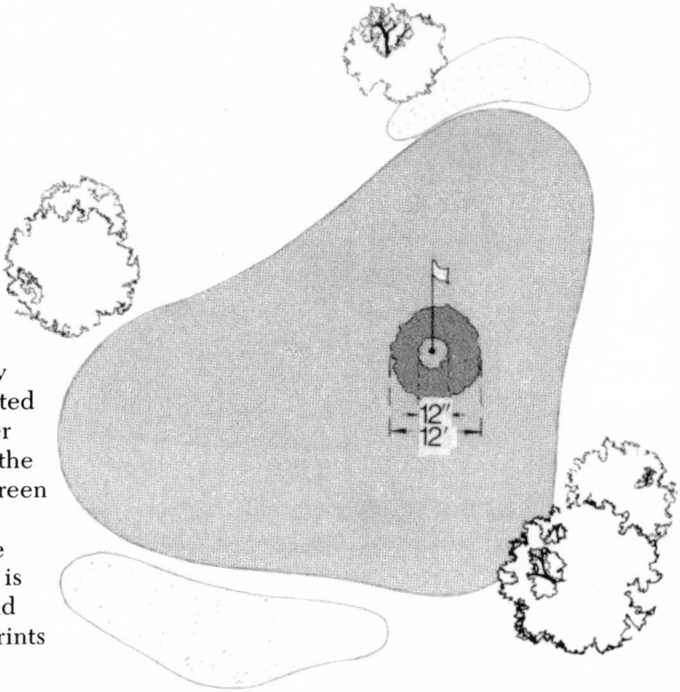

FIGURE 5.5: The "lumpy doughnut" of concentrated footprints has a diameter of about 12 feet around the cup. The more play a green receives, the "lumpier" the doughnut area. The "hole in the doughnut" is the 12-inch circle around the cup where no footprints are planted.

Keep in mind that if you have a short putt from within the "lumpy doughnut," there's a good chance your ball stopped in, and is sitting in, a footprint (Figure 5.6). A golf ball will always obey the law of gravity and come to rest at the lowest point available. And when you stroke this short putt, you won't be starting it with very much speed. So the

FIGURE 5.6: For short putts from the "lumpy doughnut" area, the ball will be sitting in a low area rather than on a peak, so the odds of getting a pure roll are decreased.

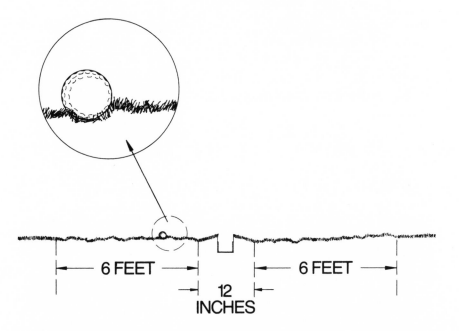

┣━━━ 6 FEET ━━━┫   ┣━━━ 6 FEET ━━━┫

┫ 12 ┣
INCHES

FIGURE 5.7: Side view of the "lumpy doughnut" shows the entrance ramp six inches on either side of the cup. A ramp can influence a weakly struck putt, causing it to veer enough to miss.

ball can easily be deflected, influenced off line in whatever direction the edge of the footprint is pointing.

THE ENTRANCE RAMP

Figure 5.7 shows the side view (ground-level) of the "lumpy doughnut" area. Notice how the area immediately around the cup is raised because golfers don't step here and press down the surface. Depending on how long the cup is left in one spot, this ramp can make it extremely difficult to sink putts. Any putt that is a shade off center is influenced to turn farther off line, and any ball rolling a bit weakly will pull up short.

After a single day of steady play, the height of the ramp from the edge of the "lumpy doughnut" to the lip of the cup may be ⅛ inch high. If the cup is left in the same spot for two days, the ramp becomes close to 3/16 inch high. If the cup is left there a week, your ball may have to traverse a ramp so severe that even casual golfers notice the incline and complain to the golf committee about "poor conditions" on the greens.

What Do the Pros Really Make?

There's a big difference, for amateur or pro, between putting a few balls on the practice green (where you repeat the putt and know the line) and putting in competition (where you read the putt once and have just one stroke at it). Figure 5.8 (page 38) shows the percentage of putts made by professionals from a variety of distances during competition. The data were taken from the PGA Tour, and represent a minimum of 100 putts for every data point on the chart. The width of the data band at any particular length of putt indicates the uncertainty, or spread, of the "make" percentage. As you can see, there is a significant difference between the best and the worst putters observed, and even the best miss frequently.

THE OVERVIEW

I hope you now see that you can't really judge how well you have stroked a putt simply by whether or not the ball rolls into the hole. If you want to learn to do anything efficiently, you must have accurate, immediate, reliable feedback as to the results of your actions. Putting on an average practice green is hardly more valuable—in terms of learning about your stroke—than putting on a gravel parking lot! For example, on a gravel lot you wouldn't have *any* idea whether there was anything right or wrong with your stroke. The bouncing and deflecting of your ball owing to the gravel and rocks would take precedence over the effects of your own stroke. So when you miss a putt, whether it's a 30-footer or a 3-footer, don't automatically accuse yourself of having taken a poor stroke. *Half of your misses probably have nothing at all to do with your stroke itself.*

It's time now for you to sit back and look at the big picture, to make certain you don't lose sight of my intent to improve your ability to make putts.

My aim in relating problems and imperfections in both balls and putting surfaces is not to discourage you. But it is of utmost importance that you truly understand the game you are playing. No one ever said the game of golf is always fair, or that all well-struck putts go in. Still, everything balances out in the long run. *There is no luck in putting. The golfer who makes the highest number of good putting strokes will make the most putts!*

You will never make as many putts as your stroke "deserves," because of the conditions under which the game of golf is played. But that's OK. That's golf; don't be put off! This is the same for everybody and is actually a blessing in disguise. If you have realistic expectations as to how many putts you can make, you won't be overly discouraged when you miss a few. And if you don't get discouraged, you can have a go at the task of improving your stroke with greater enthusiasm. And, finally, you will know that when you improve your ability to stroke good putts, you *will* make more of those rascals!

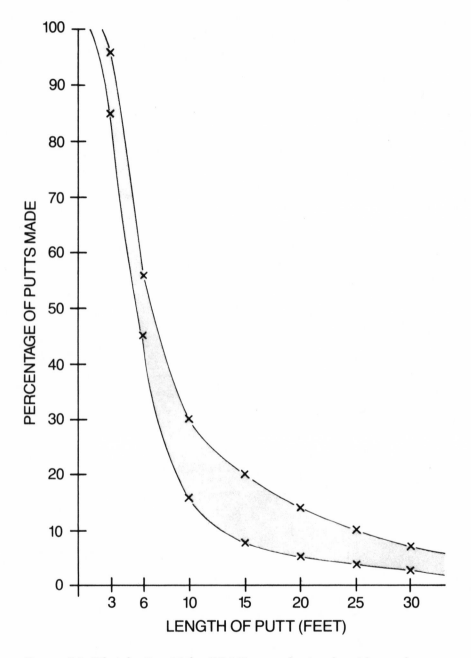

FIGURE 5.8: What the Pros Make. PGA Tour professionals, with one chance to read and stroke a putt during tournament play, sink these percentages of putts from the distances shown.

PART II: The Mechanics of Putting

6 Key Concepts of Putting

I have no intention of turning this book into a dictionary. However, it is important to briefly define some terms I will be using in the remainder of the book. I have learned through my seminars and Short Game Schools that some putting catchwords I use don't always convey the same meaning to all golfers. Let me avoid any misunderstandings right now by defining the following terms.

Target Line and Ball Line. If you ask golfers what a "target line" means in putting, they will probably say it is the line the ball rolls along toward the hole. What they are thinking of isn't the target line but, rather, the ball line. The target line is something entirely different.

The target line is always a straight line. If the putt has any break to it at all, the target line will extend from the point where the ball is sitting before you stroke it in a straight line toward an imaginary hole that I call the "secondary target." This secondary target sits to one side or the other of the actual hole. For example, if you have a putt that breaks 12 inches to the right, your target line will extend straight out toward a point that is 12 inches to the left of your actual target, the hole itself.

It is important to think of a separate and distinct target line for every putt you strike. Once you establish how much a putt will break and how hard to stroke it, align yourself to your target line. Your "job" is to make a stroke that starts the ball rolling along your target line at the proper speed. Later on in its course, the ball will take the break, allowing it to turn into the cup.

The left-hand side of Figure 6.1 shows the relationship of the target line to the ball line on putts that roll straight; in

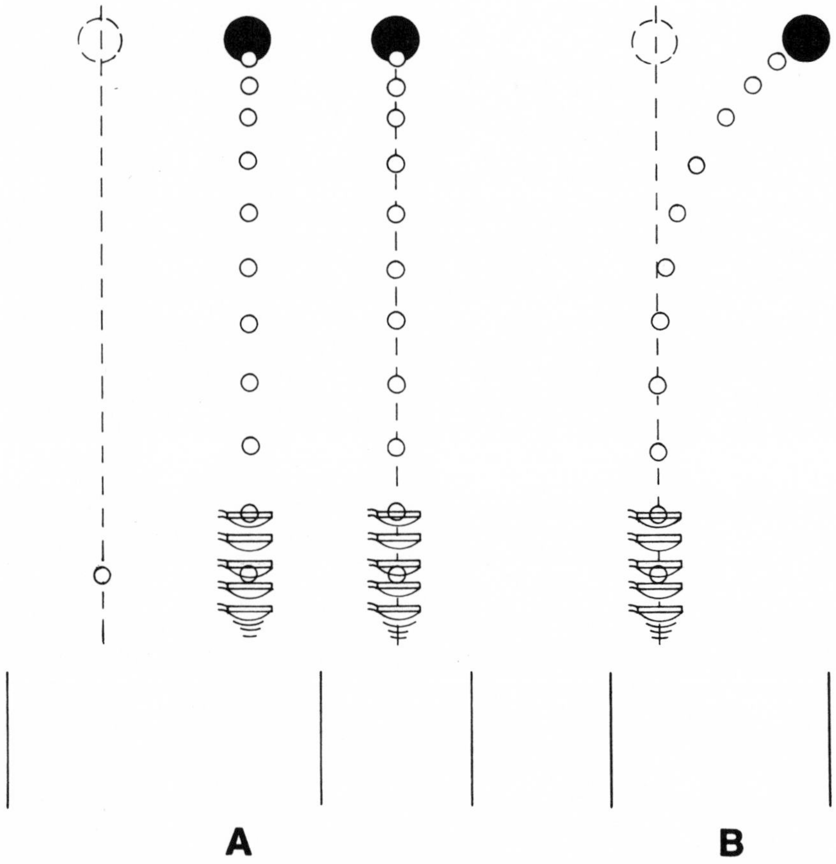

A　　　　　　　　　　　　　**B**

FIGURE 6.1: (A) For a dead-straight putt, the target line and the ball line appear to be identical. (B) For a right-breaking putt, the target line runs left of the hole by the amount the putt will break; the ball line is a curved path the ball will take to the cup.

this case the lines are identical! Now you might ask yourself, "Why should I worry about a target line separate from a ball line when they might be the same?" The answer is that for at least 90 percent of your putts, there will be some break and, thus, your target line will almost always be separate from your ball line. So you should align and start your putts along your target line on every putt. In the rare instance in which the putt is straight, your job is that much easier.

The right-hand side of Figure 6.1 shows the relationship of the target line and secondary target to the ball line and the real hole, for a putt breaking to the right. Remember, you should always try to stroke the ball along your target line and trust that your "read" (discussed in Chapter 15) allows for the right amount of break to turn the ball into the cup.

Putter Path. I define the path of the putter as the direction of motion of the putterhead relative to the target line. Usually when I talk about putter path, I refer to the putterhead's motion at one of three points in the stroke: (1) at the top of the backstroke, (2) at impact, and (3) at the completion of the follow-through. The putterhead can move *inside* (to the golfer's side) of the target line, *along* the target line, or *outside* (on the far side) of the target line. So if a player's stroke moves inside the target line going back, along the target line at impact, and back to the inside on the follow-through, then I would describe the path as "inside to along to inside."

There are almost as many putter paths as there are golfers. The path can be in a straight line either along or at various angles to the target line, it can be a curved path, it can contain various types of looping actions, or it can be a combination of all the above. From my observations, the most common path is one in which the putterhead moves back along the target line, usually a trifle inside or outside it. But as the player's stroke changes direction, he or she pushes the blade away to the outside. The putter path on the throughstroke, then, ends up being outside to inside. This is the path shown in Figure 6.2.

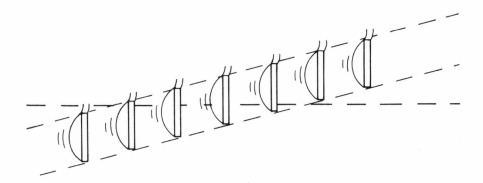

FIGURE 6.2: The putter path that moves on the downstroke from "outside to inside" the target line is the most common.

Most golfer's putter paths finish dramatically to the left, inside the target line. Many players, even some Tour pros, make a false move to bring the blade back onto the target line at the completion of the stroke. This move has no bearing on where the ball goes. The ball is already on its way. The move simply helps the golfer feel as though he or she is keeping the putter on the target line.

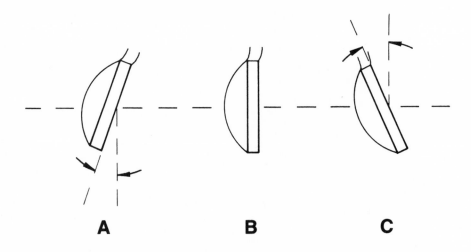

A   **B**   **C**

FIGURE 6.3: An open face angle (A) points to the right of the target line; a square clubface (B) is precisely perpendicular to the target line; and a closed clubface (C) points to the left of the target line.

Face Angle. Figure 6.3 shows the three types of face angles, or the angle between the putterface and the target line. An *open* clubface points at an angle to the right of the target line, a *square* clubface points directly along the target line, and a *closed* clubface points at an angle to the left of the target line (for right-handed golfers).

It is important to realize that face angle is always judged in this book *relative to the target line.* There is a second definition of face angle, used widely by golf professionals, in which the angle is judged relative to the direction of the clubhead's path. This definition grew out of the necessity to describe clubface positions at various points during the full swing. However, the putting stroke is much shorter than the full swing. And because the putter path moves along or very close to the target line throughout the stroke, the face angle needs to be measured and thought of in relation to the target line.

Impact Point. The impact point refers simply to the spot on the putterface where the club makes contact with the ball. Figure 6.4 shows three different impact points. The left shows the point toward the heel of the putter and the right, toward the toe. The center drawing shows contact at the center of percussion, or sweet spot, of the putter (the percussion center and sweet spot are discussed more fully in Chapters 9 and 16).

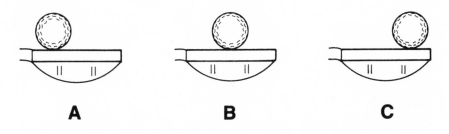

A   **B**   **C**

FIGURE 6.4: Many golfers strike the ball consistently toward the heel (A) or the toe (C); impact at the club's center of percussion, or sweet spot (B), provides the most efficient energy transfer.

THE PELZ PUTTING "PACKAGE"

The putter path, face angle, and impact point are three fundamentals of putting stroke mechanics and comprise three of the five aspects of putting that I teach. The fourth part of my system consists of your touch, your ability to stroke your putt the desired distance, and also your mind's ability to visualize the proper ball path for your putt.

Part five of my system involves your mind and the mental aspects of putting. You may have heard from time to time of a great player who can "will" the ball into the hole. I have yet to see a golfer move the ball with his or her mind (they all seem to use their putters)! Yet I don't want you to think the mind is not important. Your mind controls your body, your body controls your putter, and your putter (along with God and the greens) controls the ball. I'll deal with your mind in Part V of this book.

In the next chapter I begin to discuss the mechanics of your stroke in detail, so that you can work toward developing a stroke that is as sound as anybody's, anywhere.

7 The First Key: Improving Your Putter Path

You should now know a bit about the vagaries of the surfaces you roll your putts on. You also know these imperfections can substantially affect your results, for better or for worse. And you know about golf balls and their possible effects on the roll as well.

Now it's time to get to the meat of the matter: How can you develop the consistently repeatable stroke that gives you the best possible chance of holing your putts?

There are three fundamentals of your putting stroke mechanics that combine to determine whether you start your putts exactly along the line or not. These elements are: (1) the path of your putterhead at impact in relation to the intended starting line, (2) the angle of your putterface at impact in relation to the intended line, and (3) the point on your putter blade that makes contact with the ball. As you will see, each of these factors intertwines with the other two, and I believe all three are so important that they deserve individual, detailed discussion.

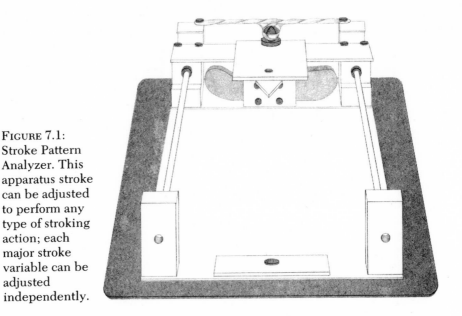

FIGURE 7.1:
Stroke Pattern
Analyzer. This
apparatus stroke
can be adjusted
to perform any
type of stroking
action; each
major stroke
variable can be
adjusted
independently.

ALL ERRORS ARE NOT EQUAL

Look at my Stroke Pattern Analyzer shown in Figure 7.1. It
uses an actual putterhead of center-shafted construction (the
shaft attaches near the blade's center rather than at one end
of the head). This is the device I use to measure the effects
of putting stroke mechanics on the roll of putts. With it I
control the path of the putter, the face angle of the blade, and
the impact point between ball and putter. During testing I
change the path the putter moves along by adjusting a single
pin. The putter path can be made to move inside to outside
or outside to inside in relation to the target line to any degree
desired, or it can move precisely along the target line. I can
adjust the face angle left or right of the target line to any
degree, or aim it dead on target. And I can set the putter to
strike the ball anywhere along the entire length of the putterhead. Bear in mind that I can adjust each element (path, face
angle, and impact point) independently of the other two.

Suppose I set the putter so its path is along the target

line, pointing straight for the hole. I aim the clubface perfectly at the target and set the ball to be struck right on the putter sweet spot. When these three fundamentals are just right, by the laws of physics the ball must start along the target line (although the ball can still be moved off line by imperfections in the green surface or poor balance in the golf ball). However, things really get interesting when I start adjusting these three stroke factors, introducing imperfections into this mechanized stroke.

Suppose you have a 20-foot putt and I want to simulate your stroke with my putting machine. When you execute your stroke I see that your path is off-line. Instead of your putter moving directly along the correct starting line to the hole, you swing in a path that is outside to inside by quite a bit—say, 10 degrees to the left of the target line. So I set the machine for the path to be 10 degrees to the left and for the face angle and impact point to be perfect.

Given this setup, how far do you think your putt will finish to the left of the hole? Most people would guess 10 degrees to the left, or approximately 2 feet off line. But they would be wrong. This putt will only roll 2 *degrees* off-line, which is only about 4 inches left of the hole. When I made actual measurements with the Stroke Pattern Analyzer I found that *only 20 percent of errors in the path of the putter are transmitted to the roll of the ball* (Figure 7.2).

These results are much, much different from the results you get if you test the path of a driver clubhead as it moves through the impact zone. When you measure a full shot such as a driver, the velocity of the clubhead at impact is very high —over 100 miles per hour for stronger players. The ball gets smashed (compressed) against the clubface, so it is forced into flight nearly along the path the clubhead is traveling (later on, it may curve right or left, but that is another story).

When you stroke a ball with a putter, however, there is very little friction, as the clubface hardly compresses the ball at all. This 20 percent path-error transmission showed up in all my tests of various putter paths, whether the path was 2

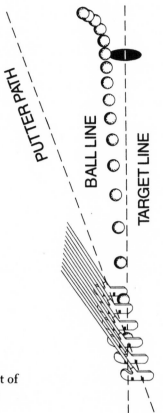

FIGURE 7.2: Path-to-Roll Relationship. Only 20 percent of any error in the stroke path is transmitted to the ball line.

degrees, 5 degrees, or 10 degrees off line—or for even larger variances in either direction.

YOU CAN SEE THE PATH

Let me ask a question. When you miss a putt to either side of the hole, what is your most likely comment? Practically without fail golfers say, "I pulled it," or, "I pushed it." You automatically assume that your putter path was off line in one direction or the other. And this might well have been the case. However, you ignore the possibility that your clubface angle or impact point could have been faulty as well.

At any rate, when you practice your stroke, what do you work on more than anything else? Why, a perfect movement of the clubhead along the target line, of course. And the reason you practice your path is that it is the only one of the three fundamentals of putting stroke mechanics that you can *see* to a reasonable degree! A friend can stand behind you on the target line and tell you, "You're cutting across it," or, "You're pushing the blade out to the right." Of course, this is merely a gross check, and it is hard to estimate the degree to which your path is off line, but the path of the clubhead is *visible* with the naked eye.

While stroke path can be assessed without the use of measurement tools, that is definitely not the case for the face angle or the point of impact between club and ball. You probably have never heard a teaching pro say, "Your clubface angle was open at impact," or "You stroked that one quite a bit away from the sweet spot of the putter." The pro cannot see those things as the stroke is occurring, so he or she deals with what can be seen—the path of the stroke.

STROKE PATH *IS* IMPORTANT

I don't want to leave the impression that putter path is not important. It is! While it is true that only 20 percent of any stroke-path error is imparted to the ball, that error alone can make you miss putts. And, inevitably, it leads to other errors in the stroke as well.

When I want to analyze a player's stroke path, I use a tool I call the Pathfinder (Figure 7.3). The Pathfinder is simply a piece of clear plastic about 1 foot long and 3 inches wide. There is a straight vertical line down its center and three horizontal lines across the bottom. I stand behind the player who is about to putt and ask where he is aiming this particular putt. If the player is aiming at the left edge of the hole, I align the center line of the Pathfinder so that it runs right through the putterface and ball, to the left edge of the

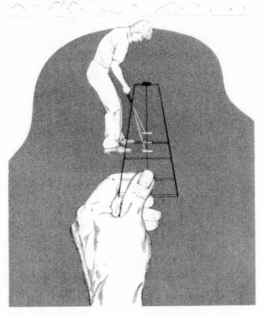

FIGURE 7.3: The Pathfinder. Watching a player's stroke through the Pathfinder makes it easy to spot both deviations in both stroke path and ball line.

hole. At this point the player strokes the ball. Since the vertical line on the Pathfinder is set directly on the perfect path, I can immediately spot any deviations in the putter path, whether the putter cut across the line, made a looping action, or whatever. I also see if the ball starts out rolling along the target line or not.

When working with PGA or LPGA Tour players, I always use the Pathfinder to evaluate the path of the stroke. I ask the player to strike five putts from 5 feet with a left-to-right break. Then I have the player strike some left-to-right—breaking 20-footers and 50-footers under the watchful eye of the Pathfinder. The player also strokes a variety of right-to-left—breaking putts and I continue to document the path of this stroke.

Usually a player's path, whether it is on the target line or off to some degree, is pretty consistent no matter what type of putt I check. In some cases though, for both Tour pros and amateurs, the stroke path *changes* depending on the type of putt! Such variances in path make it extremely difficult to putt well consistently, because it means the player must make individual, compensating motions for an erratic stroke path, from one putt to the next.

HOW TO ACQUIRE A PERFECT PATH

Now that you understand that a consistent on-line path at impact is one of the building blocks of good putting, you need to know *how* to achieve it. I'd like to tell you about my Putting Track, which I believe is the best instrument for ingraining a proper stroke path into your muscle memory.

The Putting Track is a very simple device (see Figure 7.4) first suggested to me by PGA Tour pro Jim Simons. It is a pair of aluminum rails within which to execute your stroke. The rails are adjustable in width so you can allow for as much clearance, or "breathing room," on either end of the putter as you want. When viewed from the side, the rails form a gradual upward curve to "contain" the stroke. They allow only a given amount of movement all the way from the top of the backstroke through the entire follow-through.

The Putting Track should be used indoors. Aim the track at an object such as a cup or an ashtray, thus giving you a target line to aim along. Then place a fairly large object such as a telephone book just beyond the end of the track. This

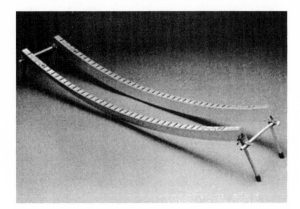

FIGURE 7.4: Overhead, side, and angled views of the Putting Track, a device that contributes to both improved stroke path and face angle.

object will immediately deflect the ball from rolling toward the target. The ball should be deflected, because this exercise is for perfecting the stroke path only. You should not be concerned with sinking the putt (or with the roll of the ball) at this point.

The goal is to move the putter back and forth in the stroke, keeping the putter between the rails without touching them or making noise at any point. It sounds really easy, doesn't it? Well, depending on how wide you have set the rails on the track, it may or may not be easy.

At any rate, the Putting Track is designed to teach you to keep the putter blade moving precisely along your target line *at the moment it makes contact with the ball*. Notice this is "at the moment of impact" rather than specifically requiring the blade to move along the target line throughout the stroke. There is a good reason for this differentiation. While the putter blade must move precisely along the target line at the point of impact with the ball, it is possible that, for some golfers, the putter not only can but *should* move on a slightly curved path during the rest of the stroke—just as the arc of the full golf swing does.

THE TRACK CAN CURVE

From what you know about the Putting Track at this point, it might appear that the track can only train you to make a stroke that stays on the target line from start to finish. And, yes, it is true that this type of path provides most golfers with the best results in the long run. However, the Putting Track can help you ingrain curved stroke paths as well.

How can a straight-railed track ingrain a "curved" stroke path? Well, notice the legs that the rails stand on. If you shorten the inside legs (legs nearest to you as you address the ball) and lengthen the outside legs, the track will tilt toward you. The rails now actually curve toward you, around your body, so they can accommodate an inside-to-square-to-inside stroke path. Adjusting the legs in the opposite manner —that is, making the outside legs shorter—curves the track away from your body, but this variation is seldom useful.

Once you set the track for the type of stroke you want to achieve, your goal is to make quiet strokes. By "quiet," I mean that the putter should not touch either of the track rails. If it does, the scraping sound of the club's toe or heel on the aluminum will be obvious! The noise provides immediate, accurate, reliable feedback on the path of your stroke. The Putting Track doesn't care who you are or how much "pressure" was on you during your stroke. And it doesn't care how many putts you would have made or missed by making a variety of other compensations in your stroke. If your putter blade moves off the desired path it will make a noise, and if the blade doesn't, it won't! The Putting Track will teach you about your stroke path and help you learn to make it more consistent, more accurate, more repeatable.

HOW "CLOSE" CAN YOU GET IT?

The degree of tolerance, or "air space," between the ends of the putter blade and the rails varies greatly depending on your ability to move the putter along a consistent path. You will need to experiment with this spacing. For starters, search for the width that allows you to make quiet strokes about 50 percent of the time. Starting with a 50 percent success rate optimizes learning. You can make this stroke successfully (quietly), but you have to concentrate and work at it to do so. Practice each stroke just as if you were putting on a real green. And stroke a ball with each setup and swing made within the track.

As you practice in the track, your path will gradually become more consistent, until you get to the point at which you can make quiet strokes about 75 or 80 percent of the time. When you get to this point, tighten the rails slightly so that you again stroke with only a 50 percent quiet rate. Do tighten the rails, because when there is no noise eight strokes out of ten, you are not getting enough feedback for optimum learning and improvement.

Some players need 1½ inches on either side of the putt-erhead and still hit the rails half the time. In this case, that is the width the player *should* begin working with. Most of you won't need quite that much room. If you consider yourself an average putter, start working with the track with 1 inch on either side of the putter blade. This setting will probably give you 50 percent quiet strokes. If you practice for fifteen minutes a day for two weeks, you should progress from 50 percent to 80 percent quiet strokes. Then move the rails to approximately a ¾-inch tolerance. After another two or three weeks, fifteen minutes of practice a day, you will probably be able to work within a ½-inch tolerance.

When you reach a success rate of 80 percent with a ½-inch tolerance, go on to the next level and allow only ¼-inch space on either side of the putter. At this point, your improvement progress from 50 to 80 percent quiet strokes will be quite a bit slower. More than likely it will take several months. That's fine. Keep working at it.

There are several PGA Tour players (Tom Jenkins, Jim Simons, and Joe Inman) who can execute their strokes within the Putting Track with only ⅛-inch tolerance on either side of the blade, yet not touch the rails nine times out of ten! That's really the best I have seen. If your stroke path ever gets anywhere near this good, you will be well on your way to becoming an excellent putter.

Just think. If the maximum path error in your stroke is ⅛ inch, it represents a very small error that your path can be off line. If you then take only 20 percent of this error (remember, that's the percentage of error transferred to the ball), you can just about stop worrying that your stroke path is causing you to miss putts. On an 8-foot putt, for example, you will never be able to notice the error this small deviation in the path can cause.

This work on your stroke path is definitely time well

spent. I can assure you that as far as my own stroke is concerned, after years of putting with the blade inside the Putting Track, I *never* have to worry about my path anymore! If you work with the Putting Track, your own path will soon be much improved as well.

REMEMBER, PATH IS JUST ONE FACTOR

The Putting Track gives you accurate feedback on your putter path. That's all. This feedback doesn't tell you if you would definitely sink the putt. It says nothing about whether you would stroke it at the proper speed for the putt at hand. It says little about your face angle and your impact point.

Still, it provides very significant information. You should work with the Putting Track for fifteen minutes a day as the starting point on your stroke-improvement program. And remember that your objective is not yet to sink putts, but to develop a consistent on-target-line-at-impact path. If you can accomplish this, you will have laid some excellent groundwork and will be on your way to an overall better putting stroke in the not-too-distant future.

With that, I'll move on to the second of the three fundamentals of putting stroke mechanics.

8 Face Angle: The Second Key for Your Stroke

I have a long-standing motto: Nobody makes just one mistake in their putting stroke. A single flaw in your stroke means missed putts. No one will consistently make the same mistake and keep missing all putts the same way. The human brain is too smart for that. As soon as it computes the fact that you are missing putts a bit to the left (because your stroke path is perhaps outside to inside), it makes an adjustment. It will probably compensate by opening the face angle of your putter. Well, while the brain is an amazing mechanism, in this instance it is about to put your putting stroke in big trouble!

In a moment I'll begin to interrelate putter path and face angle and show you why two wrongs don't make a right in terms of putting mechanics. First, however, you need to know the significance of the effect of face angle on your putts.

A 90 PERCENT INFLUENCE

I said in the last chapter that most golfers concentrate on keeping the path of the putter on target, which of course is

58

desirable. However, you can practice your stroke path until it is perfect, but if the angle of your clubface isn't also perfect, you won't make much of anything.

No one can actually see the angle of the putter face as it contacts the ball. Is it perfectly square to the target line? Is it open? Or closed? If you want to actually see the results of your face angle in action, you can manipulate the putterface severely open and your putt will shoot away to the right. Or you can close it sharply at impact so your ball rolls severely to the left. But if you are actually trying to make a putt, and you have a modicum of putting ability, any face-angle variations will be tiny, too small for your eye to catch or judge accurately. Since no one can see the face angle at impact, almost no one practices correcting it. This is one big reason why putting practice historically has never done much good.

As with my tests on the putter path, I used my Stroke Pattern Analyzer to measure putts stroked with the putterface open or closed by various degrees, testing hundreds of putts at each clubface position. And I found that with the other stroke variables constant, 90 percent of any error in clubface angle was transmitted to the ball line (see Figure 8.1). In putting, the ball starts essentially toward where the clubface is *aiming,* not along the path the putterface is moving!

Why is the ball influenced so much more by the clubface angle than by the path? Basically, it is owing to the physics of impact. There is very little friction between the putterhead and the ball at very low impact energies. This means the ball isn't "gripped," or compressed on the face, and thus is not carried along the path of the stroke to any great degree. Instead, the ball moves out in the general direction the clubface is pointing—more like the result of a collision of billiard balls than like a driver impacting a golf ball.

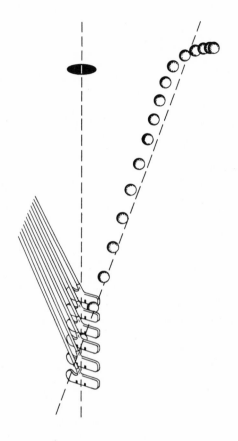

FIGURE 8.1: Face Angle-to-Roll Relationship. Ninety percent of any misalignment of the face angle is transmitted to the ball line.

TREAT STROKE PATH AND CLUBFACE ANGLE AS "EQUALS"

Most golfers I tell about the widely differing physical influences of face angle and stroke path (remember, 90 percent transfer for face-angle errors, 20 percent transfer for path errors) have the same reaction. They say, "If face angle is so much more important than path, I'd better work on my face angle and forget the path."

At this point I want to explain why this conclusion is dangerous. In Figure 7.2 you saw a path that cuts across the ball. If you were to strike every putt with that stroke path and all other parameters were in order, you would miss every putt to the left—maybe not by much, but most putts would definitely wind up to the left.

However, nobody has exactly this type of stroke. Perhaps you did have it when you first started playing golf. You may have struck your first thirty putts that way because it was your natural, instinctive stroke. But as soon as you recognized that you were missing left, you started doing something with your muscles subconsciously to open your blade a little bit and get the ball to go more on line.

Making a compensation such as this is dangerous because you will never be able to achieve the right amount of compensation repeatedly. Great putters make *consistently fewer and smaller compensations* in their strokes than do average or poor putters. So if your stroke includes a bad path, you will develop a bad face angle to compensate for it. If you start off with an inaccurate face angle at address, you are sure to develop a bad path to compensate. Maybe this doesn't sound like too big a problem for you. But we come full circle to the problem of the widely differing degrees of influence on the ball that the stroke path and the face angle impart.

I have watched hundreds of golfers exhibit stroke paths that travel to the left of where they want to aim. When I ask them what their most frequent putting problem is, almost all of them say it is missing putts to the *right!* My research has shown time and again that when a player's stroke path points left of the target, invariably *he or she misses putts to the right*. It is very simple. At one point these golfers were missing putts to the left, but they were smart enough to recognize that. Then they developed face-angle adjustments that "overpowered" the stroke-path error and now their putts keep rolling off line to the right!

By the same token, golfers who push putts to the right with a path error make subconscious adjustments by closing their face angle at impact and eventually develop patterns of missed putts to the left. However, by far the most common flaw I see is stroke path left, face angle right and putts that are generally missed to the right.

In addition, golfers who putt with this "cut" stroke and open face often are short with their putts, or strike lots of putts that barely reach the hole as they tail off to the right. The reason is that they're not striking their putts solidly. The path to the left plus the face angle to the right combine to make for a more oblique contact toward the toe of the putter. Less energy is imparted to the ball compared to the energy imparted by a square clubface and an on-line path.

So don't be too concerned with the fact that the ball responds more strongly to face-angle errors than to errors in path. Invariably, it's a case of one error leading to another, and then the results are never consistently good. You must learn to keep both factors on target from now on.

HOW TO PLAY WITH A "STRAIGHT FACE"

Without the right tools, it is virtually impossible to determine by yourself exactly where your clubface is pointing as it makes contact with the ball. Two practice aids I have developed help gauge this angle and let you straighten out any errors. One is more or less a gross check; the other measures face angle to within fractions of a degree. Let me tell you about both.

Take a look at the Putting Track shown in Figure 8.2. Notice that across the top flanges of the rails there are small lines perpendicular to the rails. These lines are spaced along the entire length of each rail. When you aim the track at an object and place your putter within it, your putterface should connect in a straight line with two lines on the rails. You will be able to see immediately if you tend to set your blade open or closed in relation to your target, because as you move toward either error, the putterface will no longer line up with those lines on the rails.

Many golfers' problems with face angle at impact stem from incorrect alignment of their putter at address. They may do nothing during the stroke to alter the face angle they start

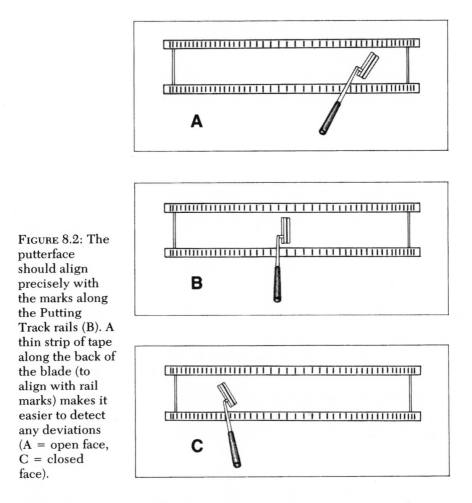

FIGURE 8.2: The putterface should align precisely with the marks along the Putting Track rails (B). A thin strip of tape along the back of the blade (to align with rail marks) makes it easier to detect any deviations (A = open face, C = closed face).

with, but for a variety of optical reasons (which vary from person to person) the blade that looks square to them really isn't.

Tour professional Jim Simons is a perfect case. When we first began working together years ago, I measured Jim's blade alignment at address on putts from various distances. I found that on a straight 3-foot putt, he aimed the putter at the left edge of the hole. On a straight 12-footer, his aim was usually dead center. Yet on a 30-footer, Simons aimed more than 3 feet to the *right* of the hole—consistently! So not only was Jim aligning the putter blade inaccurately, he was aligning it differently on different lengths of putts. Obviously he needed a tremendous athletic performance to sink putts consistently, because he had to put a different stroke on every putt to overcome these wide variations in alignment. And he putted much better when he worked this error out of his putting.

So the face angle at address is crucial. When working in the track, it may help to put a line across the top of your putter blade to let you more closely correlate the angle of the blade with the track's marks and to align exactly perpendicular to the target line. Although using the marks on the Putting Track is not a perfectly accurate gauge of the squareness of your clubface, it is a big help to most players.

The lines on the rails can also help you judge the face angle throughout your stroke, as well as at address. Occasionally, as you execute your stroke, watch the putter blade and see how far it deviates, if at all, from the track lines at the top of your backswing and at the end of your follow-through. Again, it is a gross check, but you will be able to tell for certain if the clubface is opening or closing in relation to the target line at any point along the stroke.

Now that you know a very basic way to keep tabs on your face angle, let me describe a more sophisticated face-angle analyzer. It's a device I call the TAC, which stands for Teacher Alignment Computer (see Figure 8.3). This device is quite small—about the size of a box of a dozen golf balls. When you turn on the TAC, an optical system inside the box focuses on your putter. The TAC indicates, by way of a light system along its top, how you are aiming the putter. Each light in the row of twenty-three atop the TAC indicates an error in clubface angle up to one-fifth of 1 degree. During your address of a putt, red lights flashing atop the TAC mean you are aiming significantly right or left of your target. Yellow lights indicate that you are aiming better, and if you see only green lights it means you are aiming quite accurately or even perfectly at the target.

When you align the blade exactly at the target, three

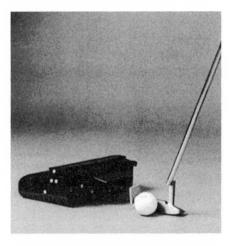

FIGURE 8.3: TAC, the Teacher Alignment Computer, tracks the putter face angle at various points in the stroke, to within one-fifth degree.

green lights in a vertical row appear, representing the perfect clubface alignment. Then as you execute your putting stroke, the TAC also measures and holds a readout of the exact angle of your putterface at the moment of impact. Technically speaking, I don't care if your face angle is 30 degrees open at the top of the backstroke or 30 degrees closed at the end of the stroke. The club doesn't influence the ball at either of those points. However, I know from the thousands of golfers I have observed that the more your clubface opens or closes during the stroke, the less likely it will be perfectly square at impact. Likewise, if you are not dead on target at address, you will have to guess or manipulate your way toward perfect squareness at impact. And these moves are both difficult to accomplish consistently.

The TAC is a tremendous visual aid in developing the muscle control needed to keep the blade square at address and at the instant of impact. Just as you "hear" stroke-path errors with the Putting Track, you "see" them with the Teacher Alignment Computer.

FORGET THE BALL

Whenever I practice with the TAC (as with the Putting Track), I don't want to see the ball roll toward a target. I put an object like a phone book or a paperweight just a few feet down the line from impact to deflect the ball. I strongly recommend that you do the same, for three reasons: (1) you should not be thinking in terms of "making" or "missing" putts while practicing face angle, (2) there is nothing convenient you can roll a ball on that is level and pure enough to give you a good enough roll to provide information regarding your stroke (and bad feedback is worse than none), (3) if you are watching the ball, you probably won't be paying attention to what you should be, which is the feel of a proper stroke, as indicated by the TAC.

My theory is simple. If you learn to aim your putter accurately at address and to keep your putterface square at impact, you will have accomplished one fundamental of the putting stroke that will serve you well. To wind up this chapter, let me advise you not to be obsessed with the devices I have discussed. You should be interested only in the feedback they provide. If you can figure out a better or easier way to learn exactly where your clubface is pointing, both at address and at impact, I say fine—use it. If it helps you conquer the second fundamental of a sound putting stroke, that's good! The third fundamental is the subject of the next chapter.

9 The Third Key: The Sweet Spot

What could be more important to good putting than moving the putter straight down the target line, with the face pointing precisely at your target? Just one little thing that very few golfers think about: striking the ball solidly.

In this chapter I talk a bit about exactly what happens when the putter strikes the ball at points other than at the putter's center of percussion, or sweet spot (the precise point at which impact will cause no rotation, turning, or wobble).

WHY "SOLID" IS SO IMPORTANT

Suppose you are moving your putter on a perfect path to the target and your face angle is exactly square to the target, but you contact the ball toward the toe of the putter. Two things happen. First, the heel of the club kicks forward. This opens the putterface so the ball starts slightly to the right of the target line. (The degree to which the ball starts off line depends on several things: how far toward the toe the impact occurs, what the weight distribution in the putter is, and how and where the shaft connects to the putterhead.)

Even more important, a percentage of the energy which should have been transferred from the putter to the ball is absorbed by the putter rotation. The result is that the ball comes off the putterface with less energy than it would have had if you had struck the putt on the blade's center of percussion.

If the ball isn't moving at quite the speed you intended it to have, it is more susceptible to break along the line of the putt. Almost every putt has some degree of break, so almost every putt rolling with less speed than planned will be affected. How much slower the ball rolls and how much more it breaks again depends on the degree to which the ball was hit off the sweet spot.

So there is no set formula for how much more a ball will break when the impact occurs away from the sweet spot of the putter. However, if you have a putt that you read to break 3 inches to the right, it doesn't take much of a "toe" hit to start the ball to the right of the intended line and have it break 6 inches instead of 3. And those differences are more than enough to cause the putt to miss the hole (see Figure 9.1).

Most amateur golfers consistently miss their putts to the "low" side of the hole. The reason is that whether the putt breaks left or right, they don't strike the putt as solidly as they had planned to. Even though they don't realize it, the impact off the sweet spot *causes* the putt to break more than anticipated. So when one of your playing partners says, "I can't believe how much that ball broke off at the end," you should remember that maybe that putt wouldn't have broken that much if it had been hit solidly on the putter's center of percussion.

Golfers who make the most putts stroke the ball on the sweet spot of the putterface. Have you ever stood by the practice green at a PGA Tour event and noticed that, when the pros stroke their putts, the ball seems to leave the blade squarely, it leaves the putter quickly, and there seems to be more energy imparted to the ball? Did you also hear a

68

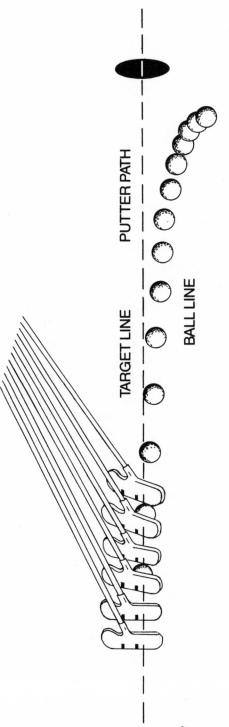

FIGURE 9.1: Impact Point-to-Roll Relationship. A ball stroked to one side of the sweet spot will start slightly off line, tend to break more, and have less energy than when struck solidly. Example shown for impact toward toe.

69

sharper sound when the putter hit the ball? Well, your senses weren't fooling you. The pros aren't putting overspin on their putts, but they *do* hit their putts more solidly than most amateurs and there is a difference in the result. But you can learn how to hit your putts just as solidly. It's really not that difficult if you have the right tools and you are willing to put in the necessary time.

HOW "SWEET" IT IS

The sweet spot, or center of percussion, on the putterface is the point at which the putter is perfectly balanced for impacting the ball. It is always located somewhere between the toe and the heel. That's not the same as saying the center of percussion is equidistant between the toe and heel. Depending on the putter's design and weight distribution, the center of percussion may be well away from the actual center of the head. The putterface will not rotate when the center of percussion strikes the ball. The blade simply slows down as it transfers the maximum amount of energy to the ball. Any time you miss this spot, you start to decrease the transfer of energy to the ball. The extreme example of poor transfer of energy is when you whiff the putt entirely!

I have compared the effect of putts struck away from the sweet spot with the results of putts struck using an incorrect stroke path or face angle. As you recall, 20 percent of the path error is transferred to the ball, as is 90 percent of the face-angle error. Impact-point errors are somewhat more complicated to measure because they transfer not only into a loss of energy (that is, loss of speed in the roll of the ball, which increases the amount of break), but also into the starting line of roll. I estimate an error-transfer efficiency of approximately 95 percent when the ball is stroked away from the sweet spot.

A "SOFT" STATISTIC THAT MATTERS

I want to interject a word of caution at this point regarding impact-error transmission to the ball. The 90 percent error transmission for putts stroked with an improper face angle and the 20 percent transmission that goes with an incorrect stroke path are what I call hard numbers. A "hard" number refers to a statistic that is measurable and repeatable—one that I can conduct a test on and prove to anyone. The 95 percent transmission for impact-point errors is what I refer to as a scientifically soft number. It is "soft" because the degree of error depends on how far you stroke the ball away from the putter's center of percussion, the weight distribution of the putter being used, and the putter's shaft axis. And the hundreds of different models of putters have different mass distributions and thus yield different results.

However, the error transmission of 95 percent for impacts off the sweet spot was the result of my testing with many common putters. For balls contacted more than ¼ inch from the sweet spot while the other parameters were in perfect order, putts of 8 feet or greater would miss 95 percent of the time. Another way to put this is that if you do everything else perfectly but miss the sweet spot by more than ¼ inch, you'll miss 95 percent of these putts.

So you see that stroking the ball on the sweet spot is tremendously important. In fact, if you had to choose among tracing a good path, using a good face angle, or striking the putt on the center of percussion (and only one of them could be just right), you should take the solid impact every time! Why? Because if you stroke the putt solidly, the ball will at least hold its line so you have a chance of its going in the hole. If you don't stroke it on the sweet spot, no matter how good your path and face angle are, the ball is going to break more than you intended and will be more responsive to the vagaries of the putting surface, too. Your chances are better with the solid strike.

71

HOW ABOUT LOCKE AND CRENSHAW?

Quite a few golfers have pointed out to me that some great putters do not stroke the ball on the sweet spot but, rather, toward the toe of the putter. A player from another era who was cited particularly for striking the ball toward the toe with tremendous success was the great South African, Bobby Locke. People ask me to explain how Bobby Locke putted so well if he didn't stroke the ball on the sweet spot.

Well, I never try to explain Bobby Locke. I never saw the man putt so I can't say whether or not he actually impacted the ball toward the toe. But if he did, and if he missed his "toe" spot once in a while like all other human beings do, then I can prove his error would have been far greater than if he had normally stroked the ball on the sweet spot and missed by the same amount. So I believe that if Bobby Locke actually struck his putts toward the toe, he would have been an even greater putter if he had struck them on the sweet spot!

People also question me about a great putter of the modern era, Ben Crenshaw, who strikes the ball toward the putter's toe as well. However, Ben tries to strike the ball consistently and solidly on the sweet spot. He is always concerned about his pace, and I believe Ben's excellent speed control and touch are the reasons that he is one of the best putters ever to play the game.

There is really no physical reason for *not* stroking the ball dead on the sweet spot of your putter. Unless you could somehow prove you are going to hit some other spot much more precisely and repeatedly, like a machine every single time, you must go with the sweet spot. You need to find the sweet spot on your putter (something I talk about in Chapter 16), then work to groove your stroke to strike your putts there.

"TEACH" YOURSELF THE SWEET SPOT

The first practical putting invention I developed back in 1974—the one that actually led to my involvement in the golf business—was the Teacher Putter mentioned in the Introduction.

The Teacher Putter (Figure 9.2) looks like a normal everyday putter, with a simple feedback device added. As you can see, there are two vertical prongs, or deflector bars,

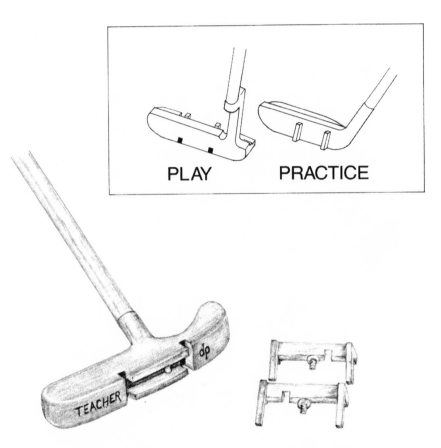

FIGURE 9.2: The Teacher Putter. This device features two prongs that frame the sweet spot and deflect any ball not struck there. Inset shows prongs in play and practice positions.

framing the sweet spot of the putter when it is ready to be used for practicing your stroke. The space between the two prongs is wide enough so that if you make a good stroke (with contact within ¼ inch of the sweet spot), the ball will roll nicely off the face as intended. If you miss the sweet spot by more than ¼ inch, instead of the putterface contacting the ball, one of the deflector bars will do so. If you strike the ball too much toward the toe, the ball will skitter to your left, off the inside of the toe prong. Strike it too much toward the heel, and the ball hits the inside of the heel prong and veers to the right. So not only does the Teacher Putter tell you that you missed the sweet spot, but you also know whether you missed it toward the toe or toward the heel (Figure 9.3).

The aspect of the Teacher Putter that I think is most important, besides the fact that it is a learning/feedback device, is that you can also use this putter *on the course itself.* You can remove the practice prongs and replace them with "playing" prongs that attach to the back of the putter instead of to the front. The "playing" prongs serve to remind you where the sweet spot is as you address the ball and that you should stroke the putt "between" the prongs even though they are really out of play.

Incidentally, I initially designed and patented the

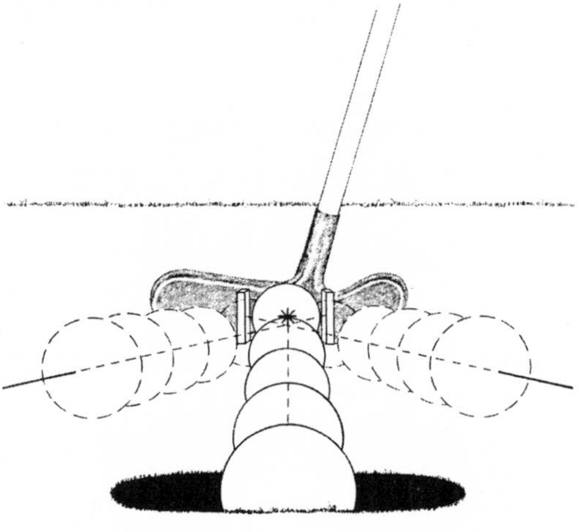

FIGURE 9.3: Putts stroked too far toward the heel of the Teacher Putter will veer right; those contacted toward the toe will move left (for right-handed putters).

Teacher Putter with a single, reversible insert; you put it on the front of the blade for practice and on the back for play. However, the U.S. Golf Association first ruled against the club, saying that it was "designed to be adjustable during play." They liked the teaching concept of the putter, though, and ruled that if a player used two separate inserts, the one on the back for play would conform to the rules and the "practice" prongs for the face of the putter would not. Of course, you'd have to be crazy to use the "illegal," or practice, insert on the course. There is no possible advantage to using the Teacher Putter in this mode for playing—only for using it to train yourself to strike the sweet spot during practice. (And I guess you have to declare before buying a putter that you're right- or left-handed so you know which insert is the legal one.) Anyway, the Teacher Putter is now an entirely legal putter for use in U.S.G.A. Rules play, and many PGA Tour tournaments have been won by players using Teacher Putters.

Another beneficial aspect of the Teacher Putter is that if you choose to play with it by using the playing prongs, it will have exactly the same weight, balance, and feel as it does in the practice mode. Two-time U.S. Open champion Andy North is a player who perfected his stroke using the practice prongs on his motel room carpet and at home. He then put the prongs on the back and competed with the same club which has exactly the same feel. Andy's stroke is now one of the most repeatable of any in the world. He has tremendous confidence that he can stroke the ball solidly. The possibility of hitting the prongs just doesn't enter his mind anymore because his stroke is absolutely under the control of his subconscious system.

Check the Tape

Sweet-spot tape is another feedback aid to help you find out where you are contacting your putts. This is a pressure-sensitive tape available in some pro shops, which you apply to the face of your putter.

If you put a piece of this tape on the putterface and strike a putt, an impression is left on the tape at the point of contact. After you putt ten or twelve times, you will see a pattern as to just how you deliver the putterface to the ball. If you have struck your putts all over the putterface, you will know that you need practice with the Teacher Putter. Likewise, you'll know if your tendency is to contact all your putts toward the toe, toward the heel, or (it is hoped) on the sweet spot.

Most of the players I have tested with sweet-spot tape show a variance of between ½ and 1 inch to either side of the putter's center of percussion. Since the amount of energy transferred to the ball goes down quite a bit once you miss the sweet spot by more than ⅛ inch, the tape shows that most players need to work on improving their ability to repeat their contact at their sweet spot.

ADJUSTMENTS TO THE TEACHER

You may recall that I said the basic Teacher Putter will tolerate a stroke that contacts the ball up to ¼ inch on either side of the sweet spot before one or the other of the prongs knocks the ball off line. At this point I should own up to an error in judgment. When I first invented the Teacher Putter, the prongs were set too close together for most golfers. I allowed a tolerance of only ⅛ inch on either side of the sweet spot. I set it that way after practicing with it for quite a while myself, and I could consistently keep the ball within the prongs. However, I quickly found this tolerance was much too tight for many golfers. Often the average players found the device so frustrating they would just give up!

So I decided that the Teacher Putter needed three different inserts that could provide reasonable tolerances for golfers with varying qualities of putting strokes. The Standard prongs allow for contact ¼ inch to either side of the sweet spot, as I have described. The Pro prongs allow ⅛ inch tolerance on either side. And the Super Pro prongs allow just ¹⁄₁₆ inch tolerance. (Some PGA Tour players call these the "North" prongs because Andy North is about the only person they know who can use them.)

GRADUATING TO A HIGHER "CLASS"

If you decide to use a Teacher Putter in your practice program, I advise you to practice with it for fifteen minutes a day. (By now I'll assume you've completed your path and face-angle improvement programs.) Start by working with the prongs that allow you to make a "successful" (no prong contact) stroke as close to 50 percent of the time as possible. More than likely, you should start off using the Standard prongs. If you start at a 50 percent "success" rate and practice for fifteen minutes a day, within two weeks you will probably reach the 80 percent success rate you should strive for when working with any feedback device.

Once you consistently stroke the ball between the prongs eight times out of ten, move to the Pro prongs with the ⅛-inch tolerance. Let me warn you that progress with the Pro prongs is quite a bit slower than with the Standard prongs. As I stated earlier, practicing within a ⅛-inch tolerance is pretty tough. You may need to work at it for several months. And you may never get to the point at which you stroke the ball purely enough that you need to move on to the Super Pro prongs. There are very few golfers who can consistently stroke their putts between the prongs of the Super Pro insert. Players like Andy North, Tom Kite, and

Bert Yancey can do it extremely well. But we're talking about the upper, upper echelon of putting strokes in the world today. These fellows are even better than the rest of the PGA Tour players.

So, to you golfers who are struggling mightily to improve your impact-point consistency by using the Teacher Putter, I congratulate you. At the same time, let me remind you that you are working with one of the most frustrating devices you will ever see. Players all assume they will be able to control their muscles during the stroke to the extent that they can impact the ball within ¼ inch of the sweet spot. Well, it just isn't so! At least, not without a lot of work.

I am not guaranteeing that you will ever become as adept as Andy North at hitting your putts on the sweet spot. But I urge you to practice with the Teacher Putter for fifteen minutes a day as the third step in your improvement program. Start with the Standard prongs and see if you can get to the point at which you can stroke "prongless" putts eight times out of ten, then go on from there. It won't take very long for you to see the improvement in your stroke, both during your practice and on your scorecard when you play.

10 Learn Your Setup from Perfy

I have talked in detail about what you need to do with your putter in terms of path, face angle, and impact point in order to develop an optimum stroke. Somewhere along the line you may have begun to say to yourself, "OK, I know what I am supposed to do with the putter. Now tell me what to do with *myself*. How should I stand to the ball, and what effects will this have on my stroke?"

I have spent many years trying to understand the relationship between a golfer's address position and the stroke characteristics that result from it. In my work with Tour pros as well as golfers of all skill levels in my Short Game Schools, I have seen a variety of different stroke movements. As a result of this experience, I know there are several alternative strokes that can work very well. And this is as good a time as any to dispel the idea that I want or expect all my pupils, or anyone who reads this book, to become clones of one particular image on the putting green. While it is true that there are a number of physical principles to which all excellent putters adhere, within that framework you can and must still develop your "own" stroke. You will see what I mean in this chapter and in the next, which provides you with a checklist for the physical factors involved in the putting stroke.

THE PROS WANTED SOME ANSWERS

As my work progressed in the late 1970s, I discovered that even among excellent PGA Tour putters, there was a great deal of variation in the way they moved the clubhead in their putting strokes. In Tom Kite's stroke, for example, the blade moved from square at address to slightly open during the backstroke, then back to more or less square at impact, before closing beyond impact. (This is probably the most common perception of the way the putterface *should* look as it moves through the stroke; in terms of the backstroke, impact, and follow-through, it was "open to square to closed.") Jim Simons, on the other hand, exhibited a very different blade movement on his putts. He managed to keep the blade square to the target line going back. Then he dropped it into an open position as he changed direction and kept it that way during the rest of the throughstroke. (In terms of backstroke, impact, and follow-through, then, Simons was "square to open to open.")

Both of these players, along with several others, asked me the questions: "What path should my putter be moving along?" and "What should my clubface angle be doing throughout the stroke?"

Back then, my answer to these questions were admittedly a bit vague. I would tell the players, "I like to see you keep the putter blade square to the target line through impact (because I had seen some great putters do that) and keep the path of your stroke close to the target line throughout." This was obviously unsatisfactory, and I remember Tom Kite's response, "*How* square? How much face-angle rotation is in the perfect stroke? How much—exactly—should I bring the putter path inside the target line? Pelz, don't tell me 'a little more' or 'a little less' of something. Tell me *exactly* what the perfect stroke is and I'll develop it!"

THE BIRTH OF PERFY

Professionals at this level of ability and intelligence don't make serious changes in their games until they know both *why* and *how* they should make them. And at that point, I really didn't have an understanding or theory as to the perfect putting stroke. But what I did have was the idea that if I could build a humanlike putting machine, it would allow me to study the mechanics of putting in detail. And with careful, precise, detailed study, I could then probably understand the "true" theory of putting.

I concentrated on a machine that duplicated the bone structure of the human body. After constructing several complex prototypes, I gradually worked my way through a simplification process which resulted in the birth of Perfy, the putting robot, shown in Figure 10.1. Perfy was manufactured from aluminum, with adjustability for length at the ankles, knees, hips, spine, and shoulders. Perfy's arms are "one piece"—that is, there are no joints to hinge at the wrists or elbows, so the swinging action Perfy performs is a pure pendulum motion.

FIGURE 10.1: I can adjust Perfy, the putting robot, to simulate the address position of any player.

In sharp contrast to earlier heavyweight prototypes, Perfy comes in weighing a nifty sixty-seven pounds (this weight is important, since airlines allow seventy pounds as a maximum weight for any suitcase). Perfy folds up and disassembles so it lives easily in a case for travel to PGA Tour stops to work with Tour pros, or to seminars for PGA golf professionals. Once out of its case, Perfy livens up our discussions of the theories of putting and how the stroke can and should be performed.

Upon achieving a workable Perfy, I adjusted it to the exact dimensions of several Tour players' arms, legs, hips, and so on. I could then see what their strokes would be like if they were to use no muscles, based on Perfy's stroke with starting positions determined by the players' own setup and stance.

The first set of tests I ran with Perfy involved Tom Kite, Allen Miller, Tom Jenkins, and Jim Simons. The results were of primary importance in developing my understanding and theory of putting, and I thank these players sincerely for their input and comments which were so instrumental to my progress. Now let me take you through some of the results from these tests.

HAND POSITION CONTROLS STROKE PATH

Where do you position your hands when you address the ball with the putter? Most players will try to answer that question while making the assumption that I am looking face-on at your address position. You might say you place your hands "directly over the ball" or "slightly ahead of the blade" or "opposite the inside of my left thigh." Which is fine, except that I am asking you where your hands are positioned in relation to your body as I look at you from "up target"—that is, from the direction of the hole. And perhaps you don't know how to answer that question because no one's ever asked it—from that perspective at least. In all the instruction you have read previously about putting, it is something that simply didn't come up, so you may not have thought about it.

As Perfy will demonstrate, *it is this position of your hands at address in relation to your shoulder sockets that determines the proper path of your stroke, as well as the angle of the blade at any point in the stroke.* I can adjust Perfy's arms so they angle out or away from its body, so they hang straight down, or so they angle in, tight to the body. The result is three different stroke paths, even though Perfy's arms move back and through in the same pendulum manner from all three positions!

Let me discuss the three types of strokes and their pluses and minuses.

THE HANDS-OUTSIDE-SHOULDERS STROKE

Years ago it seemed that everyone I talked putting with believed that the "correct" or "natural" putting stroke was one in which the putter path moved from inside to square to inside, with the clubface rotating from open to square to closed relative to the target line. After all, these people reasoned, this is what happens in the full golf swing, and the putting stroke is really a miniature golf swing. Figure 10.2 demonstrates by Perfy this movement of the pendulum-type stroke, which emanates naturally from this hands-outside-shoulders address position.

The hands-outside-shoulders position is fine if it feels comfortable for you and you execute the mechanics properly, returning the clubface through the ball square to your target line and moving along that line in the zone of impact. There are pitfalls to this hands-outside-shoulders stroke, however. Many golfers have a tendency to exaggerate the amount they move the clubhead inside the target line going back. The more inside the line this movement is, the more the clubface will open and the more the clubhead will need to rotate

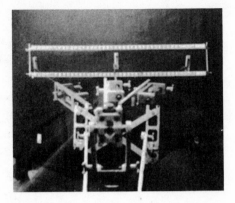

FIGURE 10.2: Hands-outside-shoulders stroke demonstrated by Perfy results in "open-square-closed" clubface movement.

counterclockwise to get back to square at impact. If you get your hands too far outside your shoulder sockets at address, you need a tremendous amount of skill to return the clubface to the ball in a square position.

This type of setup can lead to another possible problem: ball position. Your ball position at address will have to be perfect, since you must contact the ball at that single position when the clubface is square to the target. If you happen to play the ball an inch too far back in your stance (an easy enough error to make) the clubface will contact the ball with a slightly open clubface. And as we know from Chapter 8, 90 percent of that clubface-angle error will be transferred to the roll of the ball. So even this tiny error might be enough to cause a miss. Conversely, if you have the ball an inch or so forward of your perfect square clubface point, the clubface will be closing and you'll miss to the left.

If you putt with your hands outside your shoulder sockets at address, it is still possible to move the blade straight back and through along the target line. However, you will have to use muscle-controlled manipulations of your hands and wrists, and there is little chance of doing that consistently. I would rather see you make a pure pendulum stroke and allow the putter to move along that inside-square-inside path, without any contributions from your hand or forearm muscles. (Don't forget that if you own a Putting Track, you can adjust it by shortening the inside legs and lengthening the outside legs so the track curves to accommodate your inside-square-inside stroke path. Just make certain you adjust the Putting Track to the stroke you want, rather than adjusting your stroke to the Putting Track!)

If you've been putting with your hands outside your shoulders and aren't getting the results you want, have a friend check your hand position from down the target line. If your hands are well outside your shoulders, I recommend moving them closer toward being directly under your shoulders. You will automatically take the club back less inside and keep the clubface a little squarer to the target line throughout. This is the suggestion I made to Peter Jacobsen, who was basically a hands-outside-shoulders putter. Peter (see Figure 10.3) now has his hands almost directly under his shoulders, and he is a more consistent putter for it.

FIGURE 10.3: Peter Jacobsen is an example of a PGA Tour player employing a hands-outside-shoulders address position.

THE HANDS-INSIDE-SHOULDERS STROKE

Look at Perfy's stroke shown in Figure 10.4. Its arm position is just the opposite of the previous one. Perfy's arms are now pinched in tight to its body. In fact, from in front or behind, you would see that its "hands" are *inside* its shoulder sockets.

Although this is the only change in Perfy's setup, the resulting difference in its putting stroke is dramatic. The "pendulum" stroke moves *outside* the target line going back, along the line at impact, then back to the *outside* in the follow-through. The clubface angle during the stroke is a bit closed going back, then square at impact and open in the follow-through. A top player who illustrates this hands-inside-shoulders position is Fuzzy Zoeller (Figure 10.5).

Your first reaction might be that this is an "oddball" kind of stroke. You see it only rarely. If your stroke looked anything like this as a beginner, a well-meaning teacher almost certainly would have discouraged you from using it, explaining that you should "never take the putter back outside the target line." This adage might explain why Zoeller actually takes the putter back to the *inside* by rotating his forearms and employing wrist action, as opposed to Perfy's pendulum stroke. Most golfers who address the ball from this position tend to do "something" to keep from swinging the club out-

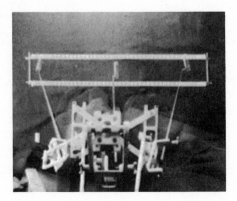

FIGURE 10.4: The hands-inside-shoulders stroke produces a closed-square-open blade movement.

FIGURE 10.5: Fuzzy Zoeller, a rare hands-inside-shoulders putter, employs a good deal of wrist motion in his stroke.

side the line. The result is usually a very complicated stroke, and not many have ever exhibited the talent Zoeller has to make it work so well.

Be that as it may, this stroke *can* be successful. Again, Perfy demonstrates a perfect pendulum with the arms generating the movement of the putter. No small muscles of the hands or fingers are involved, so repeatability is good. It is simply the difference in the address position that generates the outside-square-outside stroke.

If you feel comfortable with your hands in the inside-the-shoulders position but aren't happy with your results, you too may be relying on the inconsistencies of wrist and forearm rotation. I would much rather see you try to make Perfy's pendulum stroke. The resulting stroke path might look funny to you, however I am certain that by using your arms and shoulders rather than the smaller muscles of your hands and wrists, you will develop a much more consistent stroke. Of course, you also must adjust your Putting Track to accommodate an outside-square-outside stroke, by length-ening the inside legs and shortening the outside legs.

By employing this hands inside your shoulders, position and a pure pendulum stroke, you are still subject to the same possibilities for inconsistency as the hands-outside-shoul-ders putter. You must contact the ball at the instant the clubface is square and moving along the target line, so the ball's position in your stance again becomes an important factor. I advise you to move your hands out from your body slightly, closer to being directly under your shoulder sockets. You'll be more consistent in the long run.

WHY THE HANDS-BELOW-SHOULDERS STROKE IS BEST

I think one of the biggest misconceptions about the putting stroke is that it is "unnatural" to keep the putter square to the target line throughout. It's "unnatural" only if you set up to the ball with your hands positioned either inside or out-side your shoulder sockets. Then you have to manipulate the putterface with your hand and wrist muscles to keep it on line, and no doubt this is difficult to do. There's a much easier way. If you set your hands *directly below your shoul-der sockets* (as Perfy is doing in Figure 10.6), the result of a pure pendulum stroke is that the putter moves straight back and straight through along the target line with the blade square to that line throughout. On the PGA Tour, Tom Wat-son is a good example of someone who uses the hands-below-shoulders setup and on-line pendulum stroke (see Figure 10.7). By the way, over the course of a career, who has made more putts than Tom Watson?

There are several advantages to setting up and stroking in Perfy's hands-below-shoulders manner. You need no wrist action to achieve an on-line path. No forearm rotation is re-quired to keep the putterface square throughout the impact zone. And if you make a slight error regarding the ball posi-tion in your stance, it won't have much effect. Your path will

FIGURE 10.6: Perfy performs the ideal "hands-below-shoulders" stroke, which results in a clubface that stays square throughout the stroke.

still be on the target line and your clubface will be square both in front of and behind your normal ball position.

In sum, I believe the hands-below-shoulders pendulum stroke is the simplest and most repeatable stroke there is. Why not develop it as your method, too?

_— P. 105 —_

SQUARE SHOULDERS: A SETUP ADVANTAGE

Several other PGA Tour players besides Tom Watson employ hands-below-shoulders, on-line strokes. Good examples are Andy North, Howard Twitty, George Archer, and D. A.

FIGURE 10.7: Tom Watson putts from the "ideal" hands-below-shoulders address position.

Weibring. Even though these players all have their hands directly under their shoulders, they do exhibit differences in individual putting postures. For example, Watson and Archer bend their elbows, while North and Weibring let their arms hang almost straight down. However, these players all have one other putting setup characteristic that I consider crucial: their shoulders are aimed *parallel to the target line.*

Shoulder Alignment Check 1

Examining your shoulder alignment outdoors is something you can do quite easily at the practice green. All you need are a friend, your putter, and two other golf clubs.

Find as straight a putt as possible. Set up to the putt and have your friend lay one club along the line to the hole, just to one side of the ball. Then ask him or her to place the second club along the inside of your shoulders and hold the club steady in that position. Step away and check if your shoulder line (as represented by the club your friend is holding) runs parallel to the left of the target line (represented by the club on the ground). If it does, great. If not, have your friend "direct" you toward the correct parallel-left shoulder position.

Learning the look and feeling of the parallel-left shoulder position is a big step toward developing an arm stroke that requires no special manipulations.

Figure 10.8 shows two golfers' setups for a straight putt. The setup on the left (A) has shoulders pointing down a line slightly left of and parallel to the target line. This parallel-left shoulder line is very important because the arms naturally tend to swing along the same line as the shoulders are aligned. If the shoulders are open in relation to the target line, as is the case with the setup on the right (B), the player is likely to swing the arms along the shoulder line, on an outside-inside stroke path. With time this open-shoulder alignment will probably lead to opening the clubface angle at impact which, as we have seen, eventually means a lot of problems to solve.

It's possible to execute an on-target stroke from an open- (or closed-) shoulder alignment, but the player will again have to manipulate the club with the forearm and/or wrist muscles to do so. Why make things difficult? Start setting your shoulders "parallel left" right now if you don't do it already.

Shoulder alignment should always remain the same, even when you are setting up to putts that break in either direction. On breaking putts, your shoulder line should be parallel left of the starting line or target line (see Figure 10.9). That is, if you read a target line that's 1 foot to the left

---

Shoulder Alignment Check 2

When you practice your alignment indoors, follow these three steps:

1. Set up to your Putting Track and get ready to stroke the ball (after first carefully aligning the Putting Track to a target).
2. Drop your putter and let your hands hang limp from your shoulders, directly below your shoulder sockets (gravity will ensure this if you simply let your arms hang with no muscle tension).
3. Point your index fingers at each other.

The line formed by your two index fingers is the line your shoulders are also aligned with! If this finger line is parallel to your Putting Track, then your shoulders are aligned perfectly. If not, just move your shoulders (keeping your arms and hands hanging limp) until your index fingers form a line parallel to your track. It's that simple!

Make it a point to check your shoulder alignment each time you set up to practice with the Putting Track.

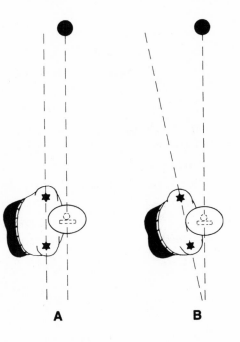

FIGURE 10.8: A parallel-left shoulder alignment (A) allows the arms to swing naturally parallel to the target line through the impact region. An open-shoulder alignment (B) requires muscle manipulation to swing the arms along the target line.

A   **B**

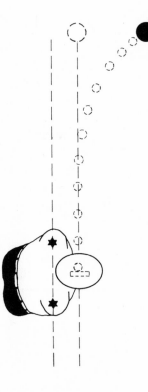

FIGURE 10.9: For breaking putts, the shoulder line should parallel the initial target line.

of the hole, try to make your shoulder line parallel the target left of line rather than parallel left of the hole itself. Then you can make your stroke without having your arms "fight" your shoulder alignment.

We have talked about what I believe are the key mechanics for a good setup and stroke. Yet there are several areas we haven't talked about that many experts regard as keys to putting—the putting grip, for example. And there are other points that I consider pertinent but which are rarely considered in putting instruction. I give you a checklist for evaluating your putting mechanics in the next chapter.

11 A Checklist for Your Putting Stroke

When I begin to work with a golfer on his or her stroke, I need to study many items to understand why the end product is as it is. Besides the three fundamentals of putting stroke mechanics I have discussed previously, there are a number of secondary factors that may or may not influence your stroke path, face angle, and impact point. All of these deserve attention.

Also, as I continue to work with a player, I find there is a constant need for re-evaluation. People and putting strokes are fluid; they change from time to time. People get bad habits without knowing it. You might have had a slight injury to your shoulder, arm, or hand that caused you to adjust your stroke at some point. Or you just might have listened to too many "hot tips" from your well-meaning playing partners and made so many adjustments that you could no longer re-member what is right. And you never got your old stroke back.

At any rate, I developed a list I call my Putting Evalua-tion Matrix. I perform this evaluation with all students when I first see them, and then update it when I see them again sometime down the road. If their putting has improved or

94

gotten worse over time, there's a reason for it and the difference shows up as a factor on the chart!

RATING THE PRIMARY VARIABLES

The Putting Evaluation Matrix shown in Figure 11.1 is a list of factors that potentially affect your putting stroke. Across the page are five spaces for comments and a numbering system running from 0 to 10 referring to the player's performance of each fundamental. For characteristics that lead to a consistent, sound stroke I fill in the left-hand side of the page

PUTTING EVALUATION MATRIX

Primary Factors

Path	Straight Along Target Line	Slight Inside Square Inside	Substantial Inside Square Inside	Inside-Out (Opposite Cut)	Outside-In (Cut)
Face Angle	Constant Square Square/Square	Small Rotation Open/Square/ Square	Symmetric Rotation Open/Square/ Open	Large Rotation Open/Square/ Closed	Hand Manipulation Very Open/ Closed/Closed
Impact Point	Sweet-Spot Repeatable	Slight Heel Repeatable	Variable Between Sweet-Spot Heel	Slight Toe	Very Toe

← CONSISTENT STROKE   VARIABLE STROKE →

FIGURE 11.1: Putting Evaluation Matrix. This organizes my evaluations of the three primary stroke factors and the secondary factors that influence the stroke. Sample comments are shown for primary factors; you can "chart" your own secondary factors.

Secondary Factors

Hand Position					
Shoulder Alignment					
Forearm Alignment					
Putter Alignment					
Ball Position vs. Apex					
Ball Position vs. Eyes					
Head Motion					
Body Motion					
Wrist Motion					
Triangle Motion					
Left Arm Swing vs. Hit					
Grip Position					
Grip Pressure					
Tempo					
Pre Shot Routine					
Attitude					
Practice Habit/Time					

and assign high rating numbers, while the movements or positions that I evaluate farthest to the right side of the page with low numbers lead to inconsistent, variable strokes. The rating system is as follows: 10 is perfect—as good as it gets, 5 is average, and 0 is the worst possible rating. If your stroke characteristics consistently merit ratings of less than 5, you've got some work to do!

The first three items on the Putting Evaluation Matrix— stroke path, face angle, and impact point—are the primary putting factors. The others are all of secondary importance in that they are important *only in how they affect the three primary factors.* If your primary factors are perfect, I would hesitate to ask you to change anything else on the list. Remember, the first three factors are what control the roll of the ball. As long as you accomplish the fundamentals, you can still be an individual on the greens to some extent!

Stroke Path. The easiest path of the putter to duplicate is the straight-back, straight-through stroke. The putterhead simply never leaves the path that runs along your target line. This is one of the paths I focused on in Chapter 7, and it rates a 10!

However, other stroke paths *can* work successfully for you. Not quite as simple, but still very viable is the stroke path that moves slightly inside the target line going back, is square to the target at impact, and then moves slightly back to the inside on the follow-through. This stroke rates an 8 on my evaluation scale. (Tom Kite is an example of a great putter who uses the inside-square-inside stroke path with success.) Next most desirable is the substantially inside-square-inside stroke. However, the more and the quicker the putter is moved inside the target line, the more important your timing becomes if you are to return the club along the target line with a perfectly square clubface at impact.

Farther to the right along our spectrum of most to least desirable stroke paths comes the inside-outside stroke path, which is the opposite of the outside-inside, or "cut," stroke.

The inside-outside path has some merit and a few professionals have been very successful with it (Bob Murphy is in the great putter category using this stroke), but I have found it hard to teach and difficult for golfers to utilize with consistent success. I really don't recommend it very often.

The worst stroke path of all—the one that appears farthest to the right on the Putting Evaluation Matrix—is the outside-inside, or "cut" stroke. While it is the most common path, it also requires the most talent to give consistently good results. If you "cut" the putter across the target line, then it becomes mandatory that you develop an open clubface at impact to compensate.

You might wonder why an outside-inside stroke, and the open clubface that results, is worse than an inside-outside stroke. I've found that golfers who have an inside-outside stroke never close the blade on their backswing to as great a degree as those with an outside-inside stroke will open it. It's simply a more difficult move to make, because natural forearm rotation on the backswing tends to open the clubface, not close it. And the less the blade moves away from "square," the better.

Face Angle. In terms of pure physics, face angle is totally independent of stroke path. But in the real world, it relates to path because, if you have a problem in one, you end up trying to compensate for it by creating a problem in the other. Chapter 8 convinced you (I hope) of how difficult this is to do.

The best face angle is the simplest one: keep it square, face angle equals zero, throughout the stroke. Although some people argue that keeping the face angle square throughout the stroke is unnatural, Perfy proves that it is both natural and easy, as do many players on the PGA Tour. So the always-square face angle rates a 10 on the evaluation chart.

The next most desirable face angle is one that rotates into a slightly open position during the backstroke, returns to square at impact, and remains square past impact. This is the stroke that a number of excellent players maintain (Tom Kite uses this now), and I think it is very good (rated 7 to 8).

Next most desirable is a symmetric rotation of the clubface from slightly open on the backstroke to square at impact to slightly closed beyond impact. This isn't bad as long as it is repeatable, and it rates about 6. But the greater the rotation from open to closed, the more important timing and ball position become and the lower the rating.

The worst face-angle behavior is one featuring independent hand manipulation to open or close the clubface in a complex or unrepeatable pattern. Obviously, you can manipulate the clubface angle with your hands in many different ways. These muscles are far too "talented" and lack the control required for your putting needs. The large muscles of your upper arms and shoulders are much more reliable. Use them instead.

Impact Point. The player who can stroke the ball repeatedly on the center of percussion (sweet spot) of the putter will get the greatest consistency of roll in terms of both distance and direction, and the highest evaluation rating.

If you had to miss the sweet spot, the next best thing would be to miss it only slightly and repeatedly. As you will see in Chapter 16, most putters are more forgiving when mishit a bit to the heel side of the blade, so it's usually best to miss in this direction.

The next best mishit pattern would be one that varies from the sweet spot to the heel of the blade. This range from sweet spot to heel is definitely preferable to hitting the ball anywhere toward the toe on most putters. Hitting the ball on the toe side of the sweet spot leads to the greatest variations in the stroke results, especially for the outside-inside cut stroke.

RATING THE SECONDARY FACTORS

Hand Position. As you've seen in the last chapter, hanging your hands directly beneath your shoulder sockets at address allows you to swing the putter back and forth along the target line with no manipulations. This hand position will automatically make your stroke more consistent and receive the highest rating.

For the next best hand position, of course I prefer to see small variations from hands-under-shoulders rather than large ones. Also, I like to see players putt with their hands outside the shoulders rather than inside the shoulders. As you have seen, players with a hands-inside-shoulders setup often use hand and wrist action in an effort not to take the putter outside the line. Since it leads to the greatest variability, I rate the hands-inside-shoulders address the least desirable.

Shoulder Line. The best shoulder alignment is one that is parallel left of your target line. It allows you to swing your arms back and forth naturally along the line of putt with no muscular compensations at all.

If I were to take Perfy onto a putting green and align its shoulders anywhere but parallel to the target line, it probably would not sink a putt. That's because Perfy has no muscle structure; it can't manipulate the club anywhere besides where it is aimed. You *can* conceivably aim your shoulders almost anywhere and then try to manipulate the putter on line based on small muscle control. But doing so definitely breeds inconsistency and low ratings.

Next to having shoulders square to the target line, I prefer to see them just slightly open. And I'd rather see players have their shoulders *very* open than to have them closed to the target line even slightly! Why? Well, when your shoulders are open, granted, you must make a muscle manipulation. However, the manipulation you need to "block" the putter toward the hole is a simple one. You can keep your hands "dead" and shove the ball toward the hole with your forearms.

If your shoulders are closed to the target line at address, invariably you will use your hand and wrist muscles in a violent attempt to roll the blade back to square to the target. That is when the serious problems start.

Forearm Position. One often overlooked setup factor that can affect the quality of the stroke is the position of the forearms when viewed from behind, along the target line. Your forearms should be even when viewed from behind—that is, your right forearm should be neither above nor below your left. Again, from this position, your bone structure encourages a straight-down-the-line stroke path with no opening or closing of the clubface.

Next best would be an address position in which your right forearm is a little lower than your left, as opposed to the right forearm being higher. When the right side is set low, it's in a less-dominant position. If you are a right-handed player, you definitely do not want your right arm set over the top of your left. A high, dominant right forearm can take over the stroke on the downswing, causing an outside-inside stroke path and a closing of the blade through impact. From the "right side low" position, it is more likely that you will err toward "blocking" your putts, the lesser of two evils.

Putter Alignment. The alignment I refer to in this chart is the accuracy with which you aim your putter down the target line at address. In my evaluation I simply measure, using my Teacher Alignment Computer, how well the player is aiming the putter.

In all the testing I have done over the years, with a range of golfers including the Tour players, the only person who has ever aimed perfectly in all of my tests is PGA Tour player Howard Twitty. He rates a 10 on my putting evaluation. D. A. Weibring is another player who is always very close to perfect alignment.

One player in particular who aimed relatively poorly is Lee Trevino. My evaluation of Lee's putter alignment was only 5, which is very poor for a Tour player. As you may be aware, Trevino aims left with his full swing (with every club in his bag), and he also aims left with his putter. He then makes an in-stroke compensation and pushes the ball toward the target. Trevino does a remarkable job in achieving a well-aligned position at impact, as is attested by his incredible record of tournament wins. However, I think Lee could have been even better if he had aimed his putter better. I believe he is the best ball striker to ever play the game.

Ball Position vs. Apex of the Stroke. This is a setup feature that receives a lot of attention for full shots, but not much when it comes to putting. Depending on the type of stroke you employ, ball position varies in importance. If you have a perfectly straight-back-straight-through stroke, in which your putterface angle is always square to your target line, ball position isn't too critical. No matter where you contact the ball during the stroke, you know the putterhead will be moving along the target line and be aimed directly at it.

Of course, it is also desirable to contact the ball at the point where the putterhead is just leaving its lowest point. This allows you to get your putts rolling smoothly and minimizes the initial backspin on your putts.

The very best ball position is about 2 inches in front of the apex, or bottom, of your stroke as shown in Figure 11.2. Where is this point in relation to your stance? For most golfers it will be slightly inside the left foot, however it is easy to measure accurately. Take your putting stance on a short pile carpet, shut your eyes, and stroke back and forth without a ball, gently lowering your stroke until the putter barely grazes the surface. Then see where this spot is in relation to your feet. Now play the ball 2 inches forward of this spot when you actually address the ball.

The next-best ball position is slightly forward or behind this optimum "2 inches forward" position in the stroke, but

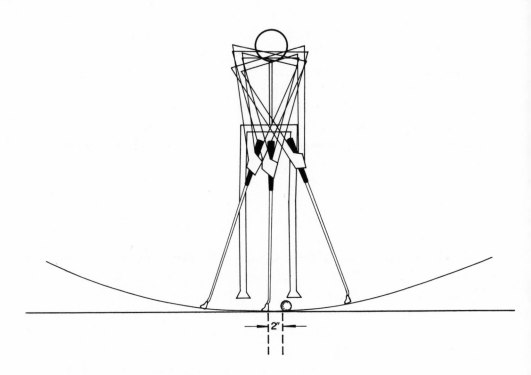

FIGURE 11.2: Ideal ball position is 2 inches in front of the lowest point in the stroke.

always in front of the arc bottom. I'd rather see you hit up on, or "top," your putts slightly, or hit them at the dead bottom of your stroke, rather than punch down on them.

Ball Position vs. Eyes. The position of the ball closer to and away from your body as it relates to the target line can be very important in relation to how you *aim* your putter. If your eyes are not directly over the target line as shown in Figure 11.3, then the apparent alignment angle between your putter blade and the target line appears to be different, based on the various distances your putts are from the hole.

I believe you can get much better at aiming and aligning your putter if the putter appears to be square to the target line no matter what the length of the putt. So if your eyes are

FIGURE 11.3: Your eyes should be directly over the target line at address. Check by holding the grip end of the putter just below your eyes: the putter should point straight down to the target line.

directly over the target line, I rate that a 10. If your eyes vary off the target line by up to 4 or 5 inches (which is often the case), my evaluation goes down to a 2 or 3.

Head Motion. The ideal motion for your head during your putting stroke is none! Actually your putting stroke rotates around a point near the bottom of your neck or your shoulder line. If you can hold your head still, the point from which the putter is being swung most certainly will stay still and will provide the most consistent and reliable motion.

My evaluation is simple in this regard: the greater the head motion, the lower the rating.

Body Motion. Your body should basically be stable and fixed from the waist down during the stroke. There usually is a small motion in the chest area owing to the rotation of the shoulders during the stroke. However, no large body motion is required since power is not the purpose of this stroke.

I certainly don't recommend any lower-body motion in the stroke. My rating evaluation for this factor is simply the more body motion, the lower the rating.

Wrist Position and Motion. The ideal wrist position is one with little or no angle between the back of your left hand and your left forearm. Also, your wrists should be arched slightly upward. During the stroke itself, the ideal is to use no wrist motion at all.

Next best would be to have a small forearm to hand angle at address, while using no wrist motion during the stroke. Tom Watson, who arches his wrists upward (and has a small forearm to hand angle) uses no wrist action during his stroke and is a good example of this. The next most acceptable combination is to have little or no angle between the left hand and forearm, but to use a little wrist motion during the stroke. Finally, setting up with a large angle between the hands and forearms (particularly with the wrists cocked downward) contributes to the very wristy stroking action, which is the least desirable of all.

Triangle Motion. When I speak of the "triangle" in the putting stroke I mean the triangle formed by the two arms and a line between the shoulders. In your putting stroke, if this triangle does not change shape, if no part of the triangle moves relative to the other parts, then you have zero motion within your triangle. The triangle swings during your putting stroke, but it should never change shape.

If there is absolutely no motion within the triangle, then rate this factor as a 10. If your elbows are straightening or bending, or if your wrists are moving back and forth, this is significant triangle motion, and I would give it a low rating.

Left Arm Swing vs. Hit. When I see a "hit" in the putting stroke, it's a very negative factor. I don't believe putts should ever be "hit." I believe they should be *stroked.* A hit implies muscular effort and muscular contractions and reactions. The

---

You Can Be a Little "Wristy" with Good Results — P. 88 —

Let me digress for a moment regarding the use of the wrists during the stroke. The wrists are largely a misunderstood item. While I do promote a "dead-hands" stroke with little or no wrist motion, I am not nearly as against the use of the wrists as people expect me to be. A slight wrist motion won't hurt your stroke *if* the following occurs: (1) your shoulders are lined up parallel to the target line, (2) your hands are under your shoulders, and (3) your stroke path moves back and forth directly along the target line. Then if you release your wrists slightly during impact, all that will happen is that the vertical arc of your stroke will become a little steeper, and the putter will move a little higher off the ground on your follow-through.

Most people think faulty wrist action is what causes them to pull putts left. Usually, though, they miss left because of excessive forearm rotation through impact. Remember that in the full swing, you rotate your forearms more than 90 degrees in both open and closed directions. It is "built into" the full shots, so many golfers do it on putts, too. Since you don't need this power move in your putting stroke, don't use it.

---

putting stroke, not being a power stroke, is much more consistently and reliably performed in a rhythmic swinging action, with no visible or measurable hit impulse occurring anywhere within the stroke.

It's easy to measure the amount of hit in a putting stroke. Address your putt normally. Before you take the putter back, however, remove your right hand from the shaft and stick it in your right-side back pocket. Now proceed with your putting stroke, controlling the putter with your left arm only.

Putt four or five balls to a hole with this motion. Repeat the left-arm-only stroke until you get the ball rolling approximately the right distance. Notice on these last few strokes how far your left forearm extends past your body on the follow-through.

Now try putting with two hands on the putter. When most golfers put their right hand on the putter and putt the same putt, making the ball roll the same distance, their follow-through is much shorter, because some of the power has been supplied from a *hit* by the right hand during impact. Their left-arm momentum then is not nearly as great. However, if the one-armed and two-armed swings are the same length for you, you have no "hit" in your putting stroke.

My evaluation of this factor is simple: the greater the "hit," the lower the rating.

Grip Position. Well, I have finally made it to a component of the putting game that you probably expected to see in Chapter 1!

If you have played the game for a while, you may have read about or tried grips such as the strong reverse overlap, weak overlap, split hand, palms opposed ten finger, double reverse overlap, and forefinger-down-shaft as illustrated in Figure 11.4. And perhaps a *dozen* other variations. Everyone wants a tip on the putting grip, because your hands and putting grip can obviously affect the manner in which you stroke the ball. But I am more interested in the *relationship of your hands to the putterface and to each other* than about whether your fingers overlap or interlock.

Whatever type of grip connection you employ, I give the highest marks if your palms face each other, with the back of the left hand and the palm of the right aligned with the putterface, perpendicular to the target line as illustrated in Figure 11.5. In addition, the ideal grip should have the club held in the *palms* of the hands rather than in the fingers.

From this position, if you can mentally visualize the back of your left hand and the palm of your right hand as aligned with —the same as or interchangeable with—your putterface, then you can efficiently keep your putterface

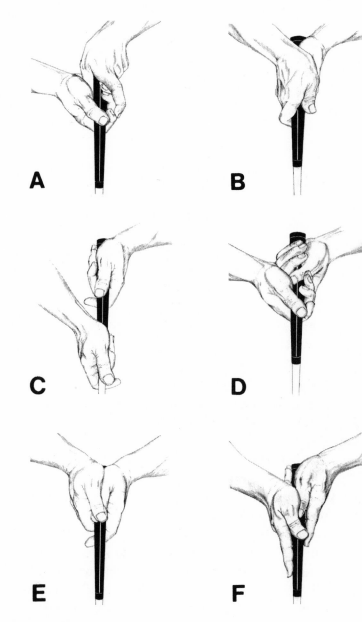

FIGURE 11.4: The grip: (A) strong reverse overlap
(B) weak overlap
(C) split hand
(D) palms opposed ten finger
(E) double reverse overlap
(F) forefinger down the shaft.

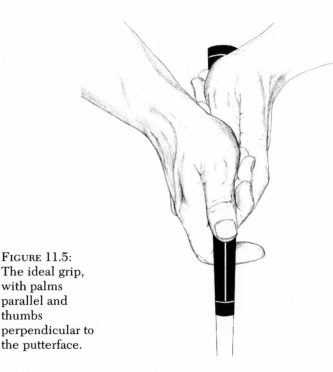

FIGURE 11.5:
The ideal grip,
with palms
parallel and
thumbs
perpendicular to
the putterface.

square to the target line. This "10-rated" grip is most easily accomplished by positioning your palms in the "parallel-to-putterface" position shown in Figure 11.6, just prior to gripping your putter.

The reason I like the club in the palms is that the more the club is in the fingers, the more "handsy" the stroke can become. In effect, with a finger grip the putter grip is farther from the "wrist hinge," so it becomes much easier to use that hinge. If the grip is in the palm, it's closer to the hinge so there is an immobilizing effect. It takes more effort to make that wrist break from this position. (I putt with the grip running up the lifeline of my left palm. Many golfers might think this is uncomfortable, that they will lose their "touch." In my own case, I had to take the hand action out of my putting stroke, and that took precedence over anything else. I simply relearned my touch by using the games I describe in Chapter 14.)

The next-best positioning in the hands is an in-the-palm

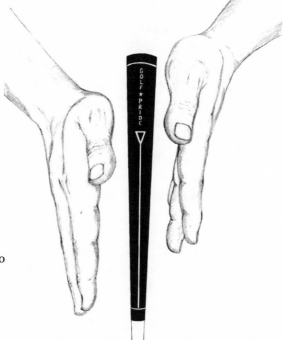

FIGURE 11.6:
Palms parallel to
putterface. This
is the best
position from
which to grip
putter.

grip with the hands in a "weak" position—that is, with the
hands turned slightly more to the left on the club. It's harder
to be "wristy" from a weak position than a strong one (hands
turned to the right). A strong grip coupled with an in-palm
position is the third-most-desirable grip.

Less desirable still is a grip in which the club is held in
the fingers. Obviously, there is a greater tendency toward
wrist action with this grip, and I rate it with low numbers.
The worst position is a "finger" grip with the hands turned
into a strong position. You'll find it difficult to execute an
arm-and-shoulder stroke and keep the blade square to the
target line with this grip.

Many golfers ask me about the different gripping techniques of split hand, cross hand and side saddle. First, I have
never seen anyone, anywhere, truly grip a putter cross-
handed. By this I mean with the hands crossed in front of the
golfer. Many golfers putt with a "left-hand-low" grip, as opposed to all the "right-hand-low" grips illustrated earlier in

Figure 11.4 (all shown for right-handed golfers). I rate the "left-hand-low" grip as a 10, an excellent grip for putting. Two of the best putters around, Bernhard Langer and Bruce Lietzke, use it with great success. The only problem I see with this grip is that most golfers who try it don't stay with it long enough to learn good touch.

As for both the split hand and side saddle grip (made famous by Sam Snead), they are both mechanically more difficult to execute than "hands together" grips. For this reason I rate them lower and don't recommend them to many players I teach.

Grip Pressure. Ben Crenshaw, one of the finest putters in the world today, holds the putter very lightly. The putter seems to me like it is almost ready to fall from his hands. Tom Watson, on the other hand, has a very tight grip; some people would even call his a "death grip" because his knuckles show white. Both men are great putters and have been for a long time, and both have one thing in common. During their strokes, at no time does their grip pressure ever change. That is the important factor of grip pressure. It is not how tightly you hold the putter, but *how consistently* you hold your grip pressure throughout your stroke. Once your putting motion is started, you must never change the pressure even the slightest amount.

If there is no change in your grip pressure, then you rate a 10. If there is a large change anywhere in the stroke, then the rating falls rapidly toward 0.

Stroke Tempo. Ideally, the stroke tempo should be smooth, flowing, and repeatable. This does not mean that you must necessarily have a *slow* putting stroke. What you need is a stroke in which the rate of movement is consistent with your personality, whether it be fast or slow. I like Lanny Wadkins' fast putting tempo as well as I like Peter Jacobsen's slow one. While both are among the elite of players in the world, Wadkins is a fast-moving, hard-driving, intense person while Jacobsen is big, slow, and laid-back. If either player tried to putt (or play golf) with the other's tempo, neither would break 80!

You should work toward a smooth, flowing, repeatable stroke tempo of your own. Don't try to mimic anybody. You have to be yourself if you are going to putt your best under pressure.

I really don't favor a player using stiff, artificial, or mechanical motions, either. Players who putt with a mechanical look never seem to reach their full potential. The human body moves best in a rhythmic, flowing manner.

That wraps up the mechanical factors you need to consider. Actually, my Putting Evaluation Matrix includes three other "nonmechanical" factors. They are the player's preshot routine, attitude toward putting, and practice habits. Attitude and practice habits are key parts of the mental side of putting and, as such, are treated in detail in Part V. The preshot routine is the subject of the next chapter.

12 How to Become a Putting Automaton

Have you ever watched a space launch, either in person or on television? It is one of the most majestic sights anywhere, a masterpiece of modern technology. And if you know how things operate during a launch, you probably know that as the prelaunch countdown draws to a close, the final sequence of events becomes automatic. As soon as the countdown reaches "T-minus 30" (thirty seconds before rocket engine ignition), the launch goes under the control of a computer. There is only one thing the human launch controller can do after that point: to stop or abort the launch.

Having been raised in the space program, so to speak, I know that whatever you want to do in the most precise, repeatable fashion is best done by committing it to computer control, to an automatic sequence of events.

DO YOU HAVE AN AUTOMATIC PUTTING ROUTINE?

I have talked in detail about the key elements of a sound stroke. You understand the need to work on imperfect mechanics that are currently part of your stroke, until you develop sufficient muscle memory and the improved stroke becomes second nature to you. Then you won't have to think about your stroke any more than you need to think about talking or breathing.

Think for a moment of your putting stroke as the "launch" of a putt. That "launch" sequence, which consists of the takeaway, impact, and follow-through, isn't something that just happens without any preparatory actions to set it in motion. At least the stroke *shouldn't* be a separate entity. Your putting stroke should have an "automatic" prelaunch sequence of events—a preshot routine—just as a space launch has.

Most amateur golfers have no prestroke routine. They step up to the ball differently every time, and commit any number of random movements which are totally different from ones they used on prior strokes. This lack of routine is a problem, because these golfers never become proficient, with repeatable or grooved actions in any one pattern or "set." And really funny things start to happen to players with no routine when they are at what I call their "pressure threshold." This is the point at which a player "feels the heat," and it varies widely from one golfer to the next. Some amateurs might reach their pressure threshold when they have a putt to break 100, or to shoot their lowest score ever. It may be on a 6-footer on the 18th green to save a $5 Nassau. Or maybe it is any short putt during a club championship match.

Whenever no-routine putters reach the point at which the pressure hits, they start doing things differently. Usually they slow down, take more time over every putt. They may "milk" the putter handle, gripping and regripping it while they stand over the ball. They might think of things they never thought before while putting. When they try to take the putter back, any rhythm and tempo they usually display is completely lost because there is no longer any subconscious control of the stroke. They are doing new things in an unfamiliar time sequence. There's no memory for the subconscious to fall back on, so nothing happens automatically. The result in these situations, when they most want to make a good stroke, is that they just can't putt at all!

A SET ROUTINE EQUALS A SET STROKE

Do you suffer from any of these symptoms? If so, it's time to improve your own putting prestroke routine. Your subconscious prestroke routine should be a functional, thought-out, systematic organization of motions that prepares you both mentally and physically for every stroke.

I have built my own prestroke and putting routine very carefully, and I can tell you that the stroke itself composes the eighth and ninth motions I make. In other words, between the time I address the ball and the moment I start to execute the actual backward stroke, there are seven other specific motions I make, the same way every time. If for any reason I can't accomplish those seven motions in a perfectly normal and rhythmic sequence, then I don't even attempt number eight. If the sequence is disturbed by an insect landing on my ball or buzzing in front of my eyes, or I feel like sneezing, or I catch myself thinking some extraneous thought, I just "abort" the process, recycle to step one, and start again.

Look at Figure 12.1, the photo of me in the putting address position. Starting with the time I assume my stance over the ball (after having taken my practice strokes), I make the following movements:

1. Shift weight to left foot, then right foot, then distribute the weight between both feet
2. Place the putter behind the ball as I look at my target
3. Wiggle my left foot until I am comfortable
4. Move my eyes from the target to the ball and focus on it
5. Regrip the putter in the lifeline of my left palm
6. Return my eyes along the target line to the target

FIGURE 12.1: My putting address position. I make a total of seven specific movements before I actually execute the stroke.

7. Look back to the ball, "forward press" my hands ½ inch toward the target and bounce the putter almost imperceptibly three times

Finally comes move number 8, when I start the putter into the backstroke. Number 9 is the impact in my forward stroke through the ball.

As you read this description of my prestroke routine, it may sound clumsy, difficult to execute, and time-consuming. You might expect me to be a candidate for slow-play penalties! Yet, if you were to watch me putt you'd get a different impression. These movements blend together into a smooth, repeatable routine that takes just eight seconds—not as long as the average player stands over the ball.

I should add here that I actually *prefer* to see players have somewhat brief routines. When you step up to the ball after your practice stroke and begin the prestroke routine, you should know exactly how you want to stroke the putt. As seconds pass, the vividness of that image of the perfect stroke begins to fade from your mind. Although I have not done this type of research myself, behavioral scientists have shown that short-term sensations (such as the image of a perfect putt) diminish by about 30 percent every eight seconds. In the next eight seconds, another 30 percent of the remaining image fades away, and so on, every eight seconds. So it's desirable to begin your preshot routine and make your stroke as soon as possible after you know what you want to do. If you are a slow-moving person like me, you may take a little longer than the next player, but don't be too concerned about it as long as you're reasonable. The most important factor is to operate within your own tempo, in a rhythmic, repeatable, automatic stroke sequence.

At any rate, you'll never see any deviation in my seven-step prestroke process. That's how automatic it is. You should *never* think about any outside details over a putt, such as how much it might be worth or what your standing is in a match. All stroke mechanics must be under subconscious control. Your prestroke routine and the stroke itself should look the same if you are putting for nothing, for a dollar, for a million dollars, or even for the lives of your children.

When I say this, I don't mean to imply that you must have nerves of steel. I simply mean that you shouldn't be able to do it any other way, even *if you tried*. In this regard, a funny thing sometimes happens when I try to show my routine to people during seminars. When I talk while I'm demonstrating, I sometimes goof up the routine. I'm not programmed to be talking (I haven't practiced while talking) in the routine, so it sometimes falls apart. In these instances, I have to shut up, recycle, and do it right!

Every player I have worked with has built a specific prestroke routine and has practiced it so much that it becomes completely ingrained in the subconscious. Some had already done so before I met them; others built it after I impressed its importance on them. None of these players looks overly mechanical during this routine. When you watch D. A. Weibring, Tom Purtzer, or Peter Jacobsen during a televised Tour event, do they look painfully mechanical in their movements? I think you'll agree they appear quite calm, composed, and in control. Their strokes emanate smoothly from the movements that precede them.

Never Stand Motionless

One specific point in the prestroke routine every golfer should work to incorporate is that of starting the putter back from the ball immediately following a final prestroke movement. There should be no halt of movement before you take your putter back. When you stand motionless time is difficult to measure, so you lose your rhythm and risk freezing over the putt. Then when you do take it back, a quick, jerky movement with the hands is more likely.

Attempt this right now in your living room. Even if you don't have your complete routine at the moment, try out a final prestroke move such as a forward press or bouncing the blade lightly, then immediately start the putter back. Your putter sole should always be off the ground and the weight of the putter should be held by your hands and arms immediately prior to your backswing takeaway.

Next try taking it back from a dead still position. Doesn't your takeaway started from a prior motion seem a lot smoother? Keep this in mind as you build your routine.

MAKE YOUR ROUTINE "TIME PROGRESSIVE"

The principle of preswing motion and rhythm is the same for both putting and full swing performance, but there is a difference between a useful sequence of motions and some motions you probably have seen in preshot routines. While he has always been a fine, fine PGA Tour player, Hubert Green used to have an incredible preshot routine for his full swing. He pumped the club up and down, the same movement over and over. That's not a helpful type of movement; it's just nervous fidgeting. In addition, Hubert stood over the ball doing this for an awfully long time, which made it more difficult to retain a clear image of what he wanted to do with the shot. Thankfully, he has since changed this preshot routine.

On the other hand, I love Lee Trevino's preshot routine. He sets the club behind the ball and as he assumes his stance, looks at his target. He looks down as he waggles the club and then looks once again at his target. Next, Trevino slides his left foot about an inch toward the target while at the same time opening his left toe a couple of inches in relation to the target line.

That movement of the left foot is Trevino's swing trigger. Once he slides the foot, the very next motion is the takeaway. He never hits the ball without the foot slide. So when the heat is on, when the pressure's the greatest, Lee does the same thing in exactly the same rhythm. He is able to hit shots that are just as excellent in the final round of the U.S. Open as he does in a casual practice session at home, because to his subconscious control system they are the same!

I recommend that every golfer build a time-progressive prestroke routine in putting, like Trevino has in his full swing. By "time-progressive" I mean that you make every movement in the routine different from the one before. Then your subconscious will know where you stand in the process and what motion to produce next.

WHAT WILL YOUR ROUTINE BE?

It is possible you can memorize the exact routine that I, Lee Trevino, or player X use, copy it exactly, and find it the perfect introduction to your best stroke. If so, great, but I don't think this is likely. My own series of movements are used for an example, not a regimen you should copy. Trying to define an exact sequence of motion for all golfers would be foolish. There are any number of different movements and time sequences you can use. My backstroke begins as a recoiling movement from the forward press and bounce of my hands and arms. But you might choose to forward press earlier in your routine, or not to use a forward press at all. Many players use an increase in their grip pressure or a regripping motion as a trigger.

While I don't want to prescribe a specific set of movements, I definitely hope the routine you adopt will match the tempo of everything else you do. If you are a quick, nervous person, don't try to follow the routine of Jack Nicklaus or Raymond Floyd. If you are large, slow-moving, or easygoing, don't try to copy Tom Watson or Lanny Wadkins. But as I said earlier, the more decisive and efficient your routine, the better you'll be able to retain the clear mental image you had when you stepped up to the putt.

Your prestroke routine isn't something you can decide on today and implement tomorrow. You need to work on it for a while. And I suggest you work on it separately from your stroke mechanics. Definitely don't work on it during actual play. Your body may get "tongue-tied" if you try to consciously work your way through eight or a dozen movements while keeping in mind your ultimate goal of sinking the putt. It's just too much to handle at once.

Whether you work on your routine indoors or on the practice green, make certain to address a golf ball and go through your actual stroke as you complete the prestroke routine. Make certain you pick a target object to look at, and a short distance down the line place a deflector which will knock the ball away (the roll of the ball is only a distraction at this point).

Depending on how much time you spend per day or per week on your prestroke routine, it may take you from one to three months before it begins to feel automatic. Most likely, you won't even realize it's becoming automatic until after it has been that way for quite a while! It took Lee Trevino years before his wonderful preshot routine became rock-solid. And Trevino has hit hundreds of thousands of golf shots in his life. Your routine may never be as good as his, but you can certainly improve yours.

WHEN IN DOUBT, STEP AWAY

Did you ever watch a playing partner prepare to putt and, somehow or other, you just knew he or she was going to miss? I'll bet 99 percent of the time you were right. By the same token, you can often tell when someone's likely to sink one.

What causes you to get these notions one way or the other? Do you have ESP? Highly unlikely. Whether you're aware of it or not, what you're noticing is the *tempo* of the individual movements in the player's prestroke routine. A well-planned routine will require good tempo in order to look right, so the golfer (as well as the viewer) can sense when it is off. You can observe your own routine and abort when necessary.

This is something that Andy North did twice on the final green during the 1978 U.S. Open at Cherry Hills in Denver, Colorado. Andy needed only a bogey to clinch the crown as he stood on the tee, but then it took him four strokes to get within 4 feet of the hole on the difficult finishing par-four. He needed a 4-footer to win. North addressed and stood over the ball in the light breeze that blew across the green. Then he stepped away, shaking his head and smiling wryly as the crowd murmured. After restudying and stepping up to the putt, he backed away again and smiled. No doubt some of the TV announcers, the crowd, and the millions watching on TV were convinced, "He's choking!"

Finally, Andy settled in for the third time and, surprisingly to many, stroked a perfect putt in the dead center of the cup to claim the first of his two U.S. Open titles. Stepping away from that putt twice and starting over was obviously a very smart move. Andy had been out of his routine and he recognized it. But he *knew* he could make that putt if he just put his "good old automatic North" stroke on it. And he was stubborn enough to get things right (get his preshot routine right) so he could do it!

A sad opposite example occurred at the final hole of the 1970 British Open at St. Andrews. Doug Sanders had brilliantly negotiated St. Andrews' befuddling Old Course for four days. He needed only a 3-footer to clinch the title over (who else?) Jack Nicklaus. The putt was no "gimme," but the key element was that midway in his prestroke routine, Sanders hesitated, stooped over, and picked a pebble out of his line. Sanders did *not* step away, however, but maintained his stance and froze over the putt even longer than normal for him.

I've heard that Ben Hogan, no stranger to the nervous strain of putting for world titles, was watching the moment on TV and yelled at Sanders on the screen, "Get away from it!" Hogan knew what was happening. Sure enough, Sanders went ahead with a feeble stroke. He knew he'd missed it the instant he hit it. You can guess who won the playoff the next day.

The lesson to learn from these two examples is this: If something is wrong with the execution of your preshot routine, *don't* try to stroke the putt, because your stroke may well be wrong, too. If you're distracted, if your motions are jerky, if the wind's blowing too hard, if a dog is barking, if you're thinking about winning or losing, or whatever, just stop and recycle. You know when you're not in your routine.

Don't go through with it. Back off! Start over! Get into the shot! Concentrate! Grind! Do whatever you have to do to do it right!

Of course, if you find yourself "out of your routine" a high percentage of the time, you know you need to put a lot more off-course effort into strengthening that routine. I know this might sound like a tedious thing to practice, and you might not even think it's that important. Believe me, it is.

You may never win or lose major championships because of the quality or consistency of your automatic preshot routine. But it will make the difference in countless small bets in your regular foursome and maybe some local tournaments as well. And I promise you: just in case you ever get the chance to putt for a major championship, it will determine your ability to "put a good move on it" when the heat is on.

So learn to be an automaton from the moment you start your prestroke routine until you've completed your stroke. Learn to think of this entire sequence as a unit, put your trust in it, be patient, and gradually you will realize you're sinking more putts.

PART III:
Feel and
Touch in
Putting

13 Why You Must Putt Boldly

I have discussed the mechanical fundamentals of your putting stroke: clubhead path, face angle, and impact point. If you have accepted everything I have said so far, you should be willing to practice indoors for fifteen minutes a day on these three fundamentals, working on each individually while getting the proper feedback. Then you can combine them and practice all three at the same time for maximum efficiency and effectiveness.

Sooner than you think, you will develop the movements of a sound, repeatable putting stroke. However, even with a stroke that is excellent mechanically, you are not quite ready to make a lion's share of putts. Why? Because up to this point you have not developed what I consider to be the fourth fundamental of good putting: touch!

In order to sink putts, you not only need to execute proper mechanics so that you start the ball precisely on the proper line to the hole. You must also have the ability to roll the ball at the proper speed, so that it holds the line you have read. As you have already learned, if you don't roll the ball at the right speed through the "lumpy doughnut," all kinds of odd things can happen to your putt.

THE CASE AGAINST LAG PUTTING

You may have previously considered the written advice of two of the greatest golfers who have ever lived, Bobby Jones and Jack Nicklaus. I have a greal deal of respect for these men both as players and as human beings. Their records are fantastic. And they could surely both beat me! But I disagree strongly with the advice they have given others regarding the speed at which you should roll your putts—namely, that you should "lag" your putts so that they die at the hole.

The Jones–Nicklaus approach (one that is also adhered to by many well-intentioned teachers) is based on the theory that a putt slightly off line can still topple in if it is just crawling to a stop as it reaches the side edge of the hole. Putting at this speed will make the hole "wider," in effect, than if your putts reach the edge while still moving with some speed.

An additional advantage to lag putting, its proponents say, is that if you should miss your first putt, the ball will finish so close to the hole that you won't have to worry about three-putting; you will only have a "gimme" left.

Sounds sensible, doesn't it? However, in this case what sounds sensible happens to be dead wrong! What lag proponents have failed to take into account is the fact that putts are not rolled over a perfectly smooth and uniform surface. As you now know, every green features a "lumpy doughnut" effect (some to a greater degree than others), and any putt over 6 inches in length must roll through this embattled area to reach the hole.

Now I am the first to admit that I had accepted the Jones–Nicklaus approach and had been a lag putter through most of my years of playing. But with the knowledge I accumulated about green surfaces, I began to wonder whether putts would hold their line better under real-life conditions if stroked at some other speed than one which would leave the ball "dead" at the hole. I decided to find out if there was a statistically more effective putting speed. Naturally, I enlisted the True Roller to help me find out.

THE "MAGIC NUMBER" FOR GOOD TOUCH

I mentioned earlier that more putts miss because of improper speed than because of improper line. If a putt is stroked too firmly, it will roll "through" the break and miss on the high side; if stroked too gently, it will break too much and miss low. Of course I wasn't interested in the speed of the putts that missed. Instead I needed to know the speed of perfect putts —those that went in. So I decided to put a "lid" on the holes being used during my testing, after the True Roller had been optimized to roll putts at the perfect "highest-probability-to-make" speed. Then I could measure the distance the ball rolled past, after it rolled over the center of the hole.

I arranged a test at a nearby golf course noted for its excellent greens. I set up and optimized the True Roller on each of the 18 greens, then measured the distance the balls rolled past the cup for putts that rolled over the hole. It turned out that in these tests, the "best" putting speed produced a distance that averaged *17 inches past* the hole!

This was terribly exciting to me. It indicated that a completely different "touch" might be the key to sinking more putts. But I wanted to make absolutely certain that this number was accurate. So shortly afterward I set up a completely different test, which would verify or refute this first test result.

This time I took data in a different manner. I set up a graph to chart the percentages of putts made by the True Roller when the putts were rolled on the optimum line for many different speeds. I tried 100 putts at each of the various speeds, for 12-foot putts with a slight break (about 3 inches). Figure 13.1 shows the complete results of the test.

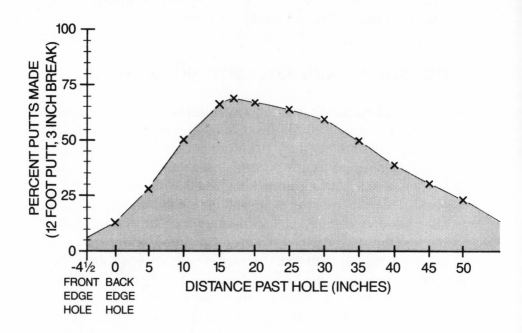

FIGURE 13.1: Percentage of putts made when rolled along the correct line at various speeds. Highest "make" percentages occur for putts rolled at a pace to stop the ball 17 inches past the cup.

After optimizing my line for my first speed, I rolled putts so they stopped just short of the front edge of the cup. On the "distance" side of the graph, this appears as minus 3 inches, meaning 3 inches short of the center of the cup. (From this group of putts, incidentally, I can safely support the statement once made by a well-known Tour pro who said, "At least 95 percent of all putts that stop short don't go in." In fact, precisely 100 percent of the putts that stopped short didn't go in!) Then I rolled putts just past the front edge, and at minus 2⅛ inches I started making putts.

Next, I rolled putts so that they died at the center of the hole. (This speed is represented by 0 inches on the chart for the distance putts rolled past the hole.) This is the perfect lag speed, as recommended by Nicklaus and Jones. But starting putts on the perfect line for this speed, the True Roller sank a mere 12 out of 100 putts! Far fewer than I had expected.

I continued setting the True Roller for the optimum line, while increasing the length of roll in 5-inch increments. At 5 inches past the center of the hole, the True Roller holed more than 25 percent of its putts. At 10 inches past, almost 50 percent of the putts went in. And at both 15 and 20 inches past the hole, about 68 percent of the putts dropped.

After the putts were rolling more than 20 inches past the center of the hole, the percentage of putts dropped. As you can see on the graph, the decrease in the percentage of holed putts occurred at a much slower rate than it had gone up, as the putts gained speed from 0 inches to plus 15 inches. The percentage stayed fairly high (although lip-outs were increasing gradually) until the putts were rolling more than 4 feet past the cup (50 inches). At that speed, the ball was almost flying over the hole and had to hit almost dead center to stay in.

So the peak on this graph shows without a doubt that the best speed at which to roll a putt in order to sink it is that speed which will carry the ball about 17 inches past the hole if it misses!

Keep in mind that 17 inches past the hole is the optimum distance no matter where you start the putt from. It can be a 3-footer, a 10-footer, a 30-footer, even a 100-footer! Rolling your putts at that speed provides the best possible combination of momentum to carry the ball unwaveringly through the "lumpy doughnut," while not moving so fast as to lip-out once it hits the hole. This maximizes the number of putts made!

WHY "17" HOLDS UP EVERYWHERE

At this point, you may have the following questions: Is 17 inches past the hole the right speed to roll the ball, regardless of the type of grass? What about the speed of the green, or whether the putt is uphill or downhill?

The answer to these questions, for all practical purposes, is yes. The 17 inches past speed is the best, most aggressive speed at which you can roll most putts on most greens.

Let's say you have an uphill putt that you sense you can go after aggressively without much fear of knocking the putt way past. If you determine to stroke this putt 17 inches past the hole, you will be stroking it pretty firmly. The ball will be moving briskly through the "lumpy doughnut," with a fair amount of steam as it reaches the hole. But the ball will come to a stop fairly quickly if it passes the hole.

On the other hand, if you have a downhill putt, you should still plan to roll it 17 inches by the hole. Because gravity is helping the ball keep rolling along its line through the "lumpy doughnut," you can get by with a putt that rolls more slowly as it passes (or goes into) the hole. The ball will still roll a little farther beyond the hole than it would at that speed if the green were level.

Following my first "optimum-speed" tests, I continued to compile research on different types of greens around the country. This research has indicated that there is indeed some variation from region to region, from course to course. On the bermuda-grass greens of Florida, with their thicker, stronger grass blades, the optimum "make" speed usually carries the ball more than *20 inches* past the hole. Indeed, the best distance can extend out as far as 36 inches on very grainy, bumpy bermuda grass. However, you shouldn't hit putts 36 inches past the hole on these types of greens; there is too great a risk of missing the putt coming back. (Give up a small percentage of your chance to one-putt, thus avoiding a possible three-putt.)

On the other side of the coin, on very smooth bent-grass

greens in the North, the right distance could be as little as 10 or 12 inches past, though that quickly increases if the greens get tracked up with footprints.

Test Your Touch

If you want to know how your present touch measures up, test yourself the next time you go to the practice green. Take a yardstick and a small notebook, along with your putter and four balls. Place one ball on each side of and equidistant from the hole, spaced round the cup in four directions. This will give you one uphill, one downhill, and two different sidehill putts.

Try to make each putt with your usual stroke. Then measure how far each putt rolls past the hole (or stops short), if it doesn't either go in or lip-out. If it does either, putt the ball again with your normal touch until you have rolled one that doesn't touch the hole.

Be certain to measure the distance the ball finishes past (or short of) the cup, as opposed to the total distance the ball finishes away from the hole. There is a big difference. A putt can finish 20 inches from the hole, but be only 6 inches past it. Measure the distance along the same line as your original putt, from the center of the cup to a point even with the ball.

Do this for each of the four putts, jotting down the number of inches each putt has gone by. Write down a negative figure for all putts that fail to reach the hole.

Go to each hole on the practice green, stroking putts of various lengths and repeating the procedure. If your practice green has nine holes, when finished you will have thirty-six measurements. Add the number of inches for all these measurements, then divide by 36. The result is the average number of inches you roll the ball past the hole—a measure of your average "touch."

This test, which takes no more than thirty minutes, shows in what direction and how much you need to "retrain" your touch.

Summing up, the 17-inch standard holds up very well, no matter where or when you might play.

WHAT THE RIGHT TOUCH CAN DO FOR YOU

How much will knowing this optimum speed help you? Possibly more than you realize!

Let's assume that you have developed a putting touch over the years with which you roll your putts—on average—5 inches past the center of the hole. Next, let's assume that you are in a putting match. You are putting against someone who putts exactly as you do—almost. Your opponent employs the exact same stroke path, the exact same face angle at impact, and he or she contacts the ball at exactly the same point on the same type of putter. Your opponent also possesses the same mental ability, the same green-reading talent—everything is the same, except that this player has learned a touch that rolls the ball, on the average, 17 inches past the hole.

You probably can already guess that you are going to lose this match. But do you realize that your opponent will sink as many as *twice* the number of putts as you on average—and probably even more than that?

Check back to Figure 13.1. On that particular green, the True Roller made an average of 25 percent when rolling putts 5 inches past the hole. Yet at speeds of both 15 and 20 inches past, the True Roller sank 68 percent—more than 2 times more. And 68 percent is over *four times* more than the percentage sunk by the golfer whose putts just reach the center of the hole! So . . . so much for what Nicklaus and Jones say about dying your putts at the hole.

However, don't be too hard on them for saying what they believe. I believed for twenty years just as they do, until I saw the True Roller data. But then I asked myself: how can Jack make so many putts and be the world's greatest player if he dies his putts at the hole? The answer is, of course, that he doesn't. If you think of all the putts he has made over the years, how many of them stopped short? Jack actually has excellent touch, and rolls almost all his putts past the hole. So do as Jack does—not as Jack says—and you will be OK! And, by the way, if you want to watch a golfer with great touch, follow Ben Crenshaw. Ben is one of the all-time best putters, maybe *the* best, because he has incredibly good touch. He always seems to roll the ball at a speed that gives it a good chance to go in.

In my experience, more golfers stroke their putts too softly than too firmly. They either get the ball to the hole on its last breath, or leave it short completely. How many times have you seen a player stroke a putt that dies ½ inch short of the cup? The player moans, "What rotten luck! I rolled an almost perfect putt and it stops a half-inch short!" In reality, that putt was more than 20 inches short of being perfect!

Now you don't want to putt the ball 4 feet past the hole, either. The percentage you make on your first putt goes down, and you will miss some of your "comebackers" to boot. Either way, though, you are wasting some—maybe a lot—of your putting talent if you don't roll your putts at a speed that takes them 17 inches past the hole.

DON'T TRY TO CHANGE OVERNIGHT

All right, you say. You're convinced. You are ready to start putting your ball 17 inches past the hole, starting with your very next round.

Well, I have a suggestion to make at this point. Wait a minute. Slow down! Whoa! Wait at least until you know about some of the possible repercussions.

Let me tell a story that will explain why changing your touch is easier said than done. Once I completed my study on the optimum putting speed, I was very excited. So excited, in fact, that I called my friend, PGA Tour pro Jim Simons, at 2 a.m. on a Friday morning.

The night I called, Simons was competing in a Tour

event. As luck would have it, he had an early morning tee-off time for Friday's second round. So he was none too thrilled to hear from me at that hour. "What are you doing, DP, calling me at 2 o'clock in the morning?" I told Jim I had some very important information, something nobody else in the world knew. "You can make at least *twice* as many putts as you are making now, simply by increasing the speed at which you roll the ball!" I announced proudly. I got him out of bed to plot the points on a graph, indicating the percentage of putts made at different speeds, just like in Figure 13.1.

After nearly two hours of discussion, Simons was pretty excited, too. "I *do* die the ball at the hole," he admitted. He had always believed in it. He said he would put my findings to work in his next round, which was only a few hours away.

The next evening I got a phone call that was a stunner. It was Simons. "I want to thank you so much, for helping me miss my first cut of the year," Jim said, sarcastically.

"Jim, what went wrong?" I asked.

Simons replied, "On the first hole, I had an eighteen-foot putt, and I remembered just what you said—roll it seventeen inches by the hole. Well, I knocked it eight feet past, and three-putted for a bogey. On the second hole, I stroked a twelve-foot putt five feet past and three-putted. Third hole, a thirty-five-foot putt, I knocked it ten feet by and chalked up my third three-putt in a row! On the fourth hole, I was so afraid of trying to putt the ball seventeen inches by that I left it four feet short—then missed that!"

All in all, Simons had three-putted *six* of the first nine greens! On the back nine, he didn't have any three-putts— by then he had stopped trying to stroke the ball 17 inches past the hole. But as far as that particular tournament was concerned, the damage was done.

Simons asked me, "Have you ever tried to putt a ball seventeen inches past the hole? I sure can't. I can only lag for the hole or send it way by. I don't have any 'in-between.'"

I answered that I hadn't actually tried to do this—only

the True Roller had. Simons replied, "Don't ever tell me to do something on Tour that you haven't tried yourself. What a disaster!"

Of course, I apologized. Simons said he understood I was theoretically correct, but also that it was just a theory and sometimes what sounds great in theory doesn't actually prove helpful in practice. (When he hung up we were still friends, believe it or not.)

This episode showed me that a little knowledge—in this case, the knowledge of the optimum speed at which a putt should roll, without knowing *how* to do it—can be a dangerous thing.

So while Simons continued playing the Tour, I went back and studied the problem of how to develop the touch needed to roll the ball at the optimum speed. And after a great deal of experimentation, I created five games designed to help you develop the optimum touch. They are the subject of the next chapter.

14 Five Games to Develop Great Touch

Think back to the very first time you went onto a putting green. You might have been a child at the time, excited by this new challenge of rolling the ball toward a hole. You held the putter awkwardly and stood over the ball, knowing you wanted to direct it at the hole but really having no idea how to go about it.

On that first putt you hit, you probably did one of two things: you either hit the ball no more than half the distance to the hole, or you knocked it past, clear off the green. It is safe to say that at that point in time you had no "touch-for-distance" whatsoever. This beginning was true for every golfer who ever picked up a putter, including Ben Crenshaw, Tom Kite, Raymond Floyd, and D. A. Weibring—the best "touch" putters in the game today.

Putting touch is not a God-given talent. It is something you learn and develop over time. Given the proper feedback, you can improve your touch dramatically in a relatively short period of time. To help you get the necessary feedback to sharpen your putting touch, I have developed five putting games: the Short-Putt Drill, the 20-Foot Drill, The Lag-Putt Drill, Safety Drawback, and Double Safety Drawback.

Before I describe these games, let me remind you that

you will benefit most by working on your touch *after* you have conquered the basics of stroke mechanics (path, face angle, and impact point). The main reason that learning good touch is often so elusive is that most golfers strive to attain it while they have too many variables in their stroke mechanics. They strike one putt toward the toe of the blade with an open face angle and the putt dies short of the hole. They stroke the next putt with the same swing energy, but strike it solidly so that it zips 6 feet past the hole. Then they moan, "I just don't have any touch at all!" Players who first obtain repeatability in their stroke mechanics, *then* start playing these games improve their touch at a rapid rate. So can you.

THE SHORT-PUTT DRILL

It is imperative that you develop complete confidence in your ability to sink short putts consistently. The best way to increase your percentage is to tap them in *firmly*—at the speed that would take the ball 17 inches past the hole if it were to miss. Use this drill regularly, keeping a firm stroke in mind, and the short ones will soon become "automatic."

Choose a direction from the cup, and stroke three balls at the hole: one from 3 feet, one from 4 feet, and one from 5 feet. Repeat this process from the other 3 sides of the cup, so you stroke a total of twelve "testers." When you have completed this cycle, repeat the cycle two more times for a total of thirty-six putts. Then set up for a "final three" putts of 3 feet from the cup. Stroke these three 3-footers, *closing your eyes* after you have lined up the putt but just before stroking it. If you make all three with your eyes closed, the drill is complete. If any of them miss, however, go back and putt one cycle of twelve putts, one 3-footer, one 4-footer, and one 5-footer from each side of the hole before trying to make three in a row with your eyes closed again.

This game puts a degree of pressure on your stroke for the final three putts, which is good! By having to perform the last three strokes with your eyes closed, you train your sub-conscious to "feel" the correct, short stroke motion and you trust your memory to control the execution of it.

If you make your final three putts on your first try, this drill should take you about ten minutes to complete. If, how-ever, you are still putting after fifteen minutes, stop and go on to another drill. It is the combination of these games and drills that teaches you the proper touch for speed, for all lengths of putts.

THE 20-FOOT DRILL

The purpose of the 20-Foot Drill is to train your subcon-scious to perform your 20-foot stroke (one of the most popular first-putt lengths in golf) at the optimum speed for making putts. The drill consists of stroking 20-foot putts in groups of three, coming from opposite directions toward the hole until you can stop ten in a row within one putter-length of the back edge of the hole, without leaving any putts short (see the "Safe Zone" in Figure 14.1, page 142).

Here are the steps to this game: First walk off a distance of 20 feet (approximately seven steps minus 1 foot) on oppo-site sides of the cup. Mark each spot with a coin. Then stroke three putts from one side, watching each putt until it stops. Measure whether each putt has rolled past the hole, yet stopped within one putter-length of the back edge of the cup. If all three pass this Safe Zone test, proceed to the coin on the opposite side of the hole and repeat the process. If any putt fails to stay within the Safe Zone, start over again from that same coin position. Keep putting in this fashion for fif-teen minutes, or until you stop ten in a row in the Safe Zone.

In order to complete this drill in less than fifteen min-utes, you must "make" ten putts in a row into the Safe Zone. Note: the tenth putt must always be from the opposite direc-tion from the ninth, to make certain you practice setting up for one try, as you must on the golf course. This is an excellent drill for touch because the pressure mounts with each stroke. Missing the Safe Zone with any putt means you have to start over. So when you make that last (tenth) putt into the Safe Zone, congratulations! You're ready to move on to another form of touch practice.

THE LAG-PUTT DRILL

From an analysis of the PGA Tour players' ability to two-putt from various putt lengths, I have established a Lag Rule for the players I work with. On all putts up to 35 feet, try to roll the ball at the optimum speed to make the putt (17 inches past). However, for putts of 40 feet or longer, lag for the hole itself.

The Lag Rule works well because it minimizes the worry of reading the line on these long putts and allows the player to concentrate on the correct speed. The drill I use to prepare players and develop their long putt touch is the Lag-Putt Drill.

The Lag Drill consists of stroking three putts each from 40, 60, then 50 feet, trying to stop the ball within 4 feet, 6 feet, and 5 feet, respectively. Repeat this sequence two more times for a total of twenty-seven lag putts, then a "final" three putts from 60 feet. If all three final putts stop within 6 feet of the hole, your lag drill is complete. If any of these three putts finishes farther than 6 feet away, you must start over on a new final three.

If you currently average two or more three-putts per round, you'll find this practice will cut down that average, and every now and then one of your lag putts will find the hole!

THE LAG-PUTT DRILL PAYS OFF

Imagine for a moment that you and I possess equal putting skills. Say that during the course of a practice session, we both could stop every lag putt within a 6-foot circle around the cup. A small percentage would drop in, simply because of the laws of geometry: the cup takes up a certain amount of space within that 6-foot circle.

Now suppose you went to work and grooved your stroke mechanics, then improved your touch via the Lag-Putt Drill. If you improved by a factor of 2, to the degree that instead of putting within a 6-foot circle, you could stop your putts within a 3-foot circle, how many more putts do you think you would sink? You would actually sink *four times* as many putts! This is a provable fact of mathematics; by improving by a factor of 2, you will make four times as many putts. (The area inside a radius of 3 feet is *four times smaller* than the area inside a 6-foot radius!) So the cup becomes four times larger on a percentage basis.

Even if you don't improve to this degree, if you can improve your touch by 10 to 20 percent, the percentage of lag putts you sink will increase significantly.

SAFETY DRAWBACK—THE BASIC GAME FOR TOUCH

My experience with Jim Simons's trying to roll his putts 17 inches past the hole taught me how difficult it is for even a professional to change his or her touch on the greens. As a result, I thought long and hard about how to teach touch. After many theoretical and on-course sessions with PGA Tour friends, we finally developed a game that is both fun to play and developmental in learning the proper touch for putts of all lengths: thus the birth of Safety Drawback.

At this point, I want to pay a special tribute to three of my best friends on Tour: Tom Jenkins, Jim Simons, and D. A. Weibring. It is largely through their efforts to learn to putt better; their open-mindedness, persistence, willingness to try one more time; their long hours on the putting greens and honest feedback (sometimes very blunt and negative) that together we developed the game Safety Drawback.

The purpose of Safety Drawback is to develop the correct subconscious instincts to stroke putts which roll at the optimum speed to make putts, in a competitive atmosphere. Safety Drawback rewards first putts that roll at the optimum speed and penalizes those that don't by means of an area behind each cup called the Safe Zone.

The rules of the game are as follows:

1. First putts which stop in the Safe Zone may be putted out from where they stop.
2. First putts which don't come to rest in the Safe Zone must be drawn back radially away from the cup *by one putter length* prior to putting again.
3. For all putts after the second putt, the ball must be drawn back away from the hole one putter length prior to putting.
4. All matches must be at least nine holes (holes may be of any length).
5. Maximum score allowed on any hole of a match, except the last hole, is 5.
6. On the last hole of a match, all balls must be putted until holed out, with no maximum on last hole score.
7. Safe Zone is defined as the area inside a line along the back edge of hole and a semicircle of one putter-length radius around behind that point (as shown in Figure 14.1).
8. A putt is defined as "in" the Safe Zone if any part of the ball is touching the line which defines the Safe Zone.

If 17 inches is to be the average distance your ball rolls past the hole, and your "short-limit" is to reach the back edge of the hole, it makes sense that the maximum distance you should be allowed to stroke the ball past the hole is 34 inches. This gives you a leeway of 17 inches on either side of the "perfect" speed. Besides being the correct border for touch on the "long" side, 34 inches is also a very convenient distance to measure on the practice green. This is because the average putter is 35 inches long. You can stick your putt-

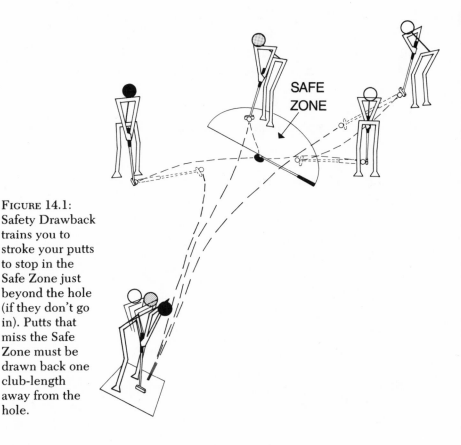

FIGURE 14.1:
Safety Drawback
trains you to
stroke your putts
to stop in the
Safe Zone just
beyond the hole
(if they don't go
in). Putts that
miss the Safe
Zone must be
drawn back one
club-length
away from the
hole.

erhead in the cup and measure 34 inches past the cup very easily.

What this boundary does is create a Safe Zone into which you want all your first putts to finish (if they don't go into the cup). And as you can see in Figure 14.1, the length of the putter is really a convenient guide to measure the Safe Zone.

It is best to play Safety Drawback with one or more opponents. Also, I believe that a small wager on the outcome is good. The greater the incentive, the more you concentrate and the more you learn! If no opponents are available, always play against your personal best score and try to lower it.

As you might imagine, with this game you could be putting for quite a while. However, Safety Drawback has a rule that the maximum score on any hole, except the last one, is 5. So if you miss your fourth putt, your fifth is "good" and you have scored the maximum. You are deemed to have "maxed-out" at 5 or, in Tour lingo, you have scored the dreaded "M–O." To keep this game exciting no matter how many strokes you might fall behind, there is no maximum score on the final hole (be it the ninth, eighteenth, or whatever) of a match. So you always have a chance to catch up on the last hole. (If you are behind starting the final hole, try to choose a difficult cup position on the side of a hill. This may cause your opponent to score a big number, and you might yet win the game!) And while you can play with first putts of any distance, I recommend you get the feel of the game with relatively short putts of less than 25 feet. As you become more proficient, you can make the game more difficult by increasing the length of some of your first putts out to the 40-foot range (but no longer, as lagging to the hole, not the Safe Zone, is in order for putts longer than 40 feet).

MAKING MORE PUTTS

You may be thinking that the main benefit of playing Safety Drawback is that it teaches you to reach the hole without going by too far, so you have an easy putt left if the first one doesn't go in. This is a benefit, but the best thing Safety Drawback does is that *it helps you sink more first putts!* If all your first putts were to finish in the Safe Zone, a higher than normal percentage will go in because: (1) they are all reaching the hole, so they *all* have a chance to go in; (2) no putts are rolling so fast that they are likely to lip-out.

I have found that Safety Drawback is a very effective practice game for all levels of players. Players focus on the most important element of putting—speed—and get good practice on short putts in the 3- to 7-foot range with the second, third, and additional putts.

DOUBLE SAFETY DRAWBACK

If you have played Safety Drawback for a couple of months and have developed what you think is a "master's" touch, you may be looking for the ultimate challenge. Try the last of my putting games, *Double* Safety Drawback. You can get an idea of what this devilish game consists of by looking at Figure 14.2.

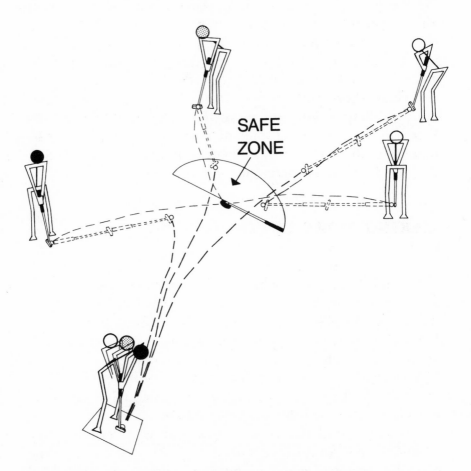

SAFE ZONE

FIGURE 14.2: In Double Safety Drawback, if the first putt misses the Safe Zone (black and white players), the player must draw the ball back *two* club-lengths from the hole. A putt stopping in Safe Zone is drawn back only one putter-length (*shaded head*).

144

The purpose of Double Safety Drawback is to develop mental toughness in putting. Double Safety Drawback is my most difficult putting game. All rules are the same as for Safety Drawback except as follows:

1. First putt stopping in Safe Zone must be drawn back one putter-length away from hole.
2. First putt stopping outside Safe Zone must be drawn back *two* putter-lengths.
3. *All* putts after second putt must be drawn back two putter-lengths prior to putting.

In Double Safety Drawback, you must make good strokes on a high percentage of your first putts and be able to hole your second putts consistently from the 3- to 6-foot range. Even if your first putt finishes within the Safe Zone, you must draw the ball back from the hole one putter-length. If you make a good stroke and your first putt just misses the hole and slips 2 feet past, the net result is that you will face a second putt of about 5 feet. Then, should you miss the 5-footer with the ball stopping 1 foot past the hole (again, a good stroke), you must draw it back two putter-lengths. And you have a 7-footer for your third putt!

If your course's practice green is reasonably challenging, with a nice combination of hole lengths and a variety of slopes, you just will not believe how difficult Double Safety Drawback can be. I have seen PGA Tour players take 12s and 14s on the final hole (26 is the Tour record on the last hole). This game can be discouraging, and it really separates the great putters from the not-so-greats. The differences between the quality of the roll of your putts and that of the next fellow's are magnified drastically.

If you are an average putter and you putt for "aces" on the practice green against a slightly better putter, or you play a match in which you putt out as you normally would during a round, with just a little good fortune you can often beat that better putter. This is because most golfers are going to two-putt most holes. If you happen to make an ace or two, you will probably win. Not so with my games, particularly Double Safety Drawback.

There is a real talent (called good touch) to stopping your first putt in the Safe Zone, which is the key to success at Double Safety Drawback. If you can do this, you automatically sink more putts to begin with. If you can make the short "testers" that follow, you are certainly the better putter. And in Double Safety Drawback, that combination allows you to slaughter your opponent.

To sum up, Double Safety Drawback is a tremendously demanding game. Please don't try it unless you have progressed well through Safety Drawback, because I don't want you to get discouraged.

HAVE YOU EVER PRACTICED TOUCH?

Even though they have tried, many golfers have never truly practiced touch in their lives! When they have a contest on the putting green, they play to lag the ball as close to the hole as possible, even from 15 or 20 feet, to ensure a two-putt. Others putt for "aces" in which their only aim is to sink the first putt. They knock the ball 3, 5, even 10 feet by, then just pick the ball up. Both of these games (particularly "aces") are *terrible* for your putting touch! They are played worldwide, yet they hurt your putting touch, rather than help it.

PLAY GAMES AND PUTT SMART

You can "damage" your touch on the course, as well. Have you ever hit a par-five green in two strokes so that you had a putt for an eagle? Invariably, one of your playing partners says, "You have a chance for an eagle; don't leave it short." You might hear the same thing if you are in a four-ball match, your partner already has a par, and you are putting for a birdie. "Whatever you do, don't leave it short!" says your helpful partner. "Give it a chance."

It used to be that whenever I found myself in one of these situations, I would end up nailing the ball about 8 feet past the hole (the Simons effect). So I just want to remind you that scooting a ball 8 feet by the hole is *not* an "aggressive" putt. It is a *dumb* putt! It has *no chance* to go in!

The smartest, most aggressive putt in golf is the one that has enough speed to roll 17 inches past the hole, then stop. Remember that, always. And the next time you go out to play, don't be too worried about "adjusting" your touch. There is a time and place for that. The time is after you have made marked improvement in your putting mechanics. Then gradually you can go out on your practice green and start working on your touch by playing these games and drills. You may even become proficient enough in touch to regularly play Double Safety Drawback. This is great fun, when you are good enough to play Double Safety Drawback and enjoy it. But, please, don't rush it.

While you are on the course, ideally you will be putting at the cup while your subconscious touch rolls your putts 17 inches by the hole. That is perfect! All you want to think about is making perfect reads and perfect strokes. And be patient with your results. If you sink the putt, well, the "lumpy doughnut" was good to you. If not, don't fret, because if you keep doing things well, you will get your rewards on the coming holes!

15

The Elusive Art of Green-Reading

How proficient are you at reading the slope, speed, and break of the greens? Excellent? Good? Just Fair? Not sure?

Most golfers can't answer this question, and perhaps no one has ever asked you before. Like almost everyone else, you've never rated your ability to judge the proper line and speed for your putts. All the time we hear a top golfer being praised for having a great swing or a pure putting stroke. But it is a rare occasion when you hear someone say, "He [or she] is really *great* at reading the greens."

To the golfer with a mediocre or poor putting stroke, being a great green-reader is not as important as it is to someone with excellent stroke mechanics. What good is it to make perfect reads on every hole if your stroke is only going to start the ball on line once in twenty tries? You might be better off if you misread more putts slightly; then, the "right" mistake in your stroke might make more balls go in the hole!

Still, the better you learn to putt, the more crucial your green-reading ability becomes. You'll need a good "read" to match that good stroke in order for the ball to drop into the cup.

GET A FAST START

Being a good green-reader requires you to judge a number of details. Not only must you gauge the degree of slope that the green's surface represents, but you must also factor in the rolling speed of the surface, the type of grass, the extent and direction of any grain in the grass, and how much any dampness might affect these factors. Sometimes you even need to consider which way and how hard the wind is blowing.

READ AS YOU WALK

The first occurs as you approach the green. It is surprising how much you can learn by increasing your awareness of the general topography as you walk up to and onto the green. For example, suppose the incline of the land of the entire hole runs decidedly from left to right, but the green looks flat. Usually this is a bit of an optical illusion, and there is probably some slope to the right in the green as well. You might not see it because of the contrast between the overall slope and the green itself.

Looking at the lay of the land as you approach the green also helps you into the green-reading mode. If you are thinking about other things until one of your partners reminds you it is your turn to putt, you may feel rushed and aren't likely to make a complete assessment. So get in the habit of paying attention *before* you get to the putting surface.

READ SLOPE FROM BELOW AND WALKING

There will never be a magic formula for determining how much a slope will make a putt break. I can't tell you, for example, that if the land along the line of a putt slopes 5 degrees to the right and the putt is 20 feet long, the ball will break 12 inches to the right. Of course, the green's slope is the primary factor in determining which way and how far the ball will roll, but many factors (discussed under "Get a Fast Start") affect the roll to varying degrees. You can study the line from the ball to the hole or, from the opposite direction, from hole to ball. Sometimes you will find a slope that looks different from one side than it does from the other. What do you do then? Well, most people have more success reading the slope from the low side, no matter which side of the hole the ball is on. By the "low" side, I mean the side the terrain is sloping down toward, so that as you look back toward the ball and the hole, you are looking *up* the slope.

If you are uncertain of the line of your putt after you have looked carefully for the slope for the low side, another way of checking is to walk from ball to hole, just to the side of your intended line. (Never walk *in* the line of your putt, because as you have seen, fresh footprints lower your chance of making the putt.) By walking alongside the line your balance system may be able to sense which way the ground is tilting.

If you still can't decide how the putt will break, you may have to make a slow circle of the hole, which is something Lee Trevino does. Circling the hole allows you to observe the line and feel the slope from all possible angles.

TO BOB OR NOT TO BOB

Another way that quite a few golfers read the slope of the green is the "plumb-bob" method. Many people are confused about what, if anything, can be accomplished with this method.

Scientifically, there is one thing plumb-bobbing can do very accurately. When you hold any putter by the butt end of the grip, it will hang down in response to the force of gravity. If the putter is properly balanced to do so, the shaft will then establish a perfect "local" vertical. If you squat down so the hole looks like a thin slit or line, you can see which way this line slopes, if any, relative to the vertical line of the putter shaft. So the plumb-bob can show you the slope of the ground at the hole, and sometimes you can see something about the slope of the green surrounding the hole also.

However, most golfers use the plumb-bob in a different way. They try to read not only which way but also *how much* a ball will break when putted toward the hole. Plumb-bobbing is not easy to do this way. The golfer attempts to use the human body as a transit, to perform a form of surveying; as such, it must be done very carefully or it can be misleading.

Most golfers stand behind the ball in a line with the hole and hold the putter up by its grip end, letting the bottom of the shaft (near the putterhead) hang down over the ball. They then shut one eye, look up at the hole, and see which side of the hole the top of the putter shaft is on. Supposedly, if the shaft appears to lie 2 inches to the left of the hole, then they contend you should aim 2 inches to the left because the putt will break that much.

However, this may not be the case. You would have to be standing precisely perpendicular to the green's sloping surface, with your stance perfectly centered along the hole-to-ball line (with your eyes positioned to the lower side of this line) for the shaft to appear to be on the upslope side of the hole. If you stand perfectly vertical, the putter shaft will cover both the ball and the cup, and you will be led to think the putt is straight. If, on the other hand, you lean your body too much against the way the slope falls, it can appear as though the ball will break *toward* what is actually the *high* side.

In other words, depending on how you stand, a putt can look like it will break three different ways! And none of this even considers how fast you intend to roll the putt, which really controls how much it will break. All things considered, I recommend great caution in plumb-bobbing your putts. It is easy to err in aligning yourself and your eyes. Even if you align perfectly, remember that you have only gained the basics of the information you need. It is knowing the total amount of break, from all factors, at the speed you are going to roll your ball, that is the real answer needed from your read.

CONCENTRATE "CLOSE TO HOME"

Whichever green-reading method you choose, remember that slopes close to the hole have more effect on the break than those farther away. The faster the ball is moving in the early part of its roll, the less the force of gravity will affect it. If the slope is constant all along the line of putt, the putt will break much more as it slows down near the hole. Also, on many well-contoured greens, you will see putts that have double or triple breaks. Obviously, you have to give more weight to the slope nearest the hole. Again, there is no mathematical formula. Every green and every putt is different. If, for example, you face a double-breaking putt that has a slope that will carry the ball to the right at first and there is an equal slope to the left in the last part of the putt, chances are the ball will break more to the left later along the line than in the first part of the roll (see Figure 15.1).

IMPROVE YOUR "SPEED READING"

Gauging the speed of greens in relation to how much the ball will break is something I can only talk about qualitatively. I can't tell you how much force you need for any given stroke to make the ball roll at the right speed to reach the hole while taking the intended amount of break. But there are some points to remember when you're "speed-reading." On a fast green, you stroke your putt with less force and the ball rolls more slowly all the way along its line. This gives the force of gravity more time to act on the ball. The faster the green, the more break you must allow.

Suppose you had two putts on exactly the same degree

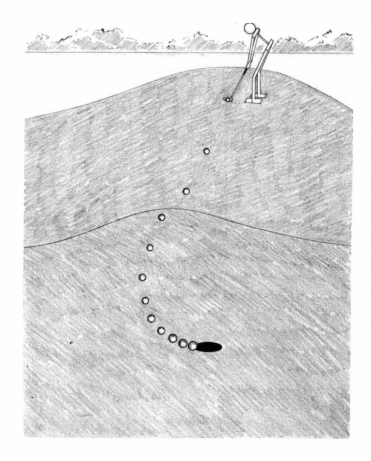

FIGURE 15.1:
Double
Breakers. For
putts that appear
to break two
ways, remember
that the ball will
be affected more
by the break
nearest the hole
because it will
have lost more
of its speed.

of slope, but they were on greens of drastically different speeds. Let's say one of the putts is on a green at Augusta National, in Georgia, at "Masters" speed. The grass is cut to ³⁄₃₂ inch, and the green measures ultrafast in rolling speed. You barely have to touch the ball to get it rolling, and it breaks about 8 feet! The other putt is on a green where the grass is ⅜ inch long. Believe it or not, you will have to stroke this putt about *five times harder,* and you will want to play less than one-third as much break as well!

Because of speed influence, green-reading becomes all the more difficult *the faster the green is.* If on a slow green you read a 4-inch break, but your read is 25 percent off, the putt will break 5 inches. You have misread by only 1 inch, so if everything else goes perfectly, you probably will still sink the putt. If, however, you are 25 percent off on a fast-green putt that breaks 20 inches, you have misread by 5 inches. So you definitely need some other "mistake" for the ball to go in the hole.

How do you judge the speed? The best way to learn how to judge the speed of greens is to stroke putts on as many different greens as you possibly can and watch the resulting rolls. Learning to read speed is basically that of cataloguing experiences you have had on greens of various speeds. Your read on any future putt is based on your memory of how the ball rolled previously, when the green looked similar. It also helps to walk along or around your line and get a feel for whether your putt will be rolling uphill or downhill and by how much. Then you can add this "plus or minus" factor to your conception of actual speed of that particular putting surface to make a final determination of how firmly to stroke the ball.

KNOW GRAIN'S "STEERING" EFFECTS

In addition to judging the rolling speed of the surface and the degree of slope, you must take the direction of the growth of the grass (grain) into account. Grain is a mystery to many amateurs. When I refer to "grain," I mean the direction the grass is growing, if it is not growing straight up (which it usually is not). If the grass is leaning predominantly toward, say, the right, then as the ball is rolling, it will tend to drift slightly in that direction. If you read a break of 6 inches to the right without the grain, then you might have to "add" 2 or 3 inches of grain break to that read. If you read the putt to break 6 inches to the left but the grain points to the right, you would subtract a small amount.

Most golfers who are aware of grain associate it with

bermuda grass only, but grain exists in bent-grass greens, too. Its effect is strongest on bermuda-grass greens because individual bermuda blades are thicker, stronger, and more wiry than more pliable bent-grass leaves. Bermuda therefore exerts more effect on the ball. A good putter considers the grain effect on all greens, not just bermuda.

Grain will affect the speed of the putt as well as the break. If you putt against the grain, the putt will be slower than usual and you must stroke more firmly to get the ball to the target. If you putt downgrain, the ball will roll faster because the cut ends of the grass blades never contact the ball. Note that when you are putting crossgrain, the ball will not only break more in the direction of the grain, but will also roll just a bit more slowly. It's the same effect as for a full shot into a crosswind, where you may need to hit one half-club extra.

GRAIN CHECKS

There are several ways to test for grain on a green. On a sunny day, judge the color of the grass from your ball to the hole. If the sun's reflection makes the grass appear whitish or shiny, it means the grain is away from you and the putt will be quicker than normal. If the grass appears dark, you are looking into the cut ends of the grass, which don't reflect as much light; the grain is against you in this case, and the putt will roll more slowly.

The faster the ball is rolling, the less the grain will affect it. Just as with the green's slope, pay the closest attention to the grain around the hole. A really strong grain factor in this area can easily turn a ball that looks to be "dead center" completely out of the hole.

Another way to determine the grain around the hole is by looking carefully at the edges of the cup. Often one side appears to be clipped clean while the other side looks a little ragged. The clean side is the side the grain is growing to-

FIGURE 15.2:
Check the Cup.
If you're putting
toward the back
of a clean-
clipped cup
edge, the putt is
against the
grain; putting
toward the back
of the rougher
cup edge means
the grain is with
you.

ward, so if you are putting toward the clean side you are putting against the grain. If, however, you are putting at the more ragged side, the grain is growing with you, and you will have to adjust your stroke accordingly (see Figure 15.2).

You can also look to some external factors to tell which way the grain is growing. Many times grass leans in the direction of a predominant wind. Also, grass always grows toward a source of water, if it is located close by. Or, in the absence of local water or predominant wind, the grass grows toward the west, toward the setting sun.

There is one method that many PGA Tour players use in practice rounds and which you can use in practice as well. Test the grain by dragging your putter lightly across the grass. If the grass blades get ruffled up, it means you are dragging the putter against the grain (see Figure 15.3). If the grass lies down, it means you've dragged the putter with the grain, flattening the blades.

You'll find that grass sometimes grows in different directions on different parts of a green. When practicing for a tournament, pros mark small arrows in their notebooks showing the direction of the grain at various locations on the green. Because they know they will see the pin in four different positions on the green during a tournament, this information usually comes in handy. Check this on your home course as well. But only test the grain with your putter during

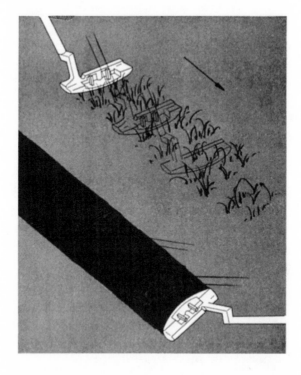

FIGURE 15.3: If dragging your putter lightly over the green lifts up tufts of grass, you're moving against the grain; you're moving the putter with the grain if it slides along the surface smoothly.

practice, never in a match (it is illegal, according to U.S.G.A. rules), and pat the grass back down after you check!

Keep in mind that putts hit with the grain break a little less than normal, as well as roll faster. Putts rolling into the grain break more, in addition to rolling slower.

DON'T FORGET WIND—AND RAIN

Not too many golfers take into account the effect of wind on the roll of a putt. You may consider wind a bother in keeping your balance while putting, but not in terms of the roll of the ball. Believe me, it can affect the roll, particularly when putting on fast greens.

At a PGA Tour event in Texas I once saw Fuzzy Zoeller running—actually running—up to a green to mark his ball. I asked him why, and he informed me he was afraid the wind would blow the ball down a slope and off the green! And at a Tour event in Florida, I watched as Payne Stewart played a 3-foot break on a 5-foot putt. Later that afternoon the same putt had a break of only a few inches. Both these players were dealing with serious wind effects on fast greens.

Using the True Roller on normal-speed greens, I have measured consistent wind effects on putts as short as 3 feet. I mention this because when you play in substantial winds —anything from 10 miles per hour on up—you should develop a "fudge factor" in your reading. Practice some straight putts with a strong breeze blowing across your line, then turn around and putt in the opposite direction. You will notice the difference.

When you play in the rain or early in the morning on dew-covered greens, you need to consider the effects of dampness. Water on the greens means your putts will break less because the grass is wet and heavy. This makes the green roll slower for putting. Of course, you will also need to stroke your putts more firmly.

Make the "Wet" Work for You

Here's a tip for playing in the rain. When you mark your ball, remove it from the surface and dry it carefully. Then replace it gently so only the small part of the ball touching the green gets wet. Concentrate on stroking the ball as squarely as possible on the line you intend, with no sidespin. If you can do this, as the ball rolls along only the center will get wet. This makes the ball heavier around its center, and it will roll straighter and truer (a gyroscopic effect). Remember to play for less break, keep your stroke firm, and use wetness to your advantage.

Practice "Reading" to Tees, Not Cups

Practice green-reading in a meaningful environment, where the quality of the putting surface is such that the ball rolls truly in terms of both speed and line. Often you won't have this when putting to cups on a putting green. Many golfers may have tracked around the holes (more so than on greens on the course), and the "lumpy doughnut" will cause the ball to roll erratically.

The solution? Stick tees in the green at various points away from the cups. Then read and stroke your putts to these tees. You will have a truer surface to read and you will get better feedback!

PUTTING YOUR "READ" TOGETHER

Your ability to read a green and then "marry your stroke" to that read is based on past experience. If you have practiced diligently and have gained from your experiences on similar greens, you should be able to stand next to your ball and execute a practice stroke that feels correct for the required putt. After the stroke, you should look up at the cup and imagine a ball rolling toward it, as if stroked by your practice swing. Learn to imagine whether the practice stroke you have taken will deliver the correct speed for the putt at hand. If you think it will roll the ball too far (instead of 17 inches past), take another stroke, using a little less swing energy.

After you execute what you perceive to be the perfect practice stroke, you can set the putter behind the ball, go into your prestroke routine, and stroke your putt with confidence. All you do at this point is reproduce your practice stroke. Don't worry about your grip, your stance, your shoulder alignment, or any of the other stroke-mechanic factors. You have taken care of these in your off-the-course practice. Now you should concentrate on executing a stroke that will propel the ball at the perfect speed to hold its line, then dive into the hole with authority!

PART IV: The Implements of Putting

16

Putter "Physics," or, What Makes a Wand Magic

The putter. The flat stick. The magic wand. It's the one club above all others that great golfers must be happy with. Many serious golfers constantly experiment, searching for the implement that will help them put the ball in the hole more often. There is no doubt that more time and mental energy are spent seeking the "perfect putter" than are consumed on all the other thirteen clubs in the bag combined.

The search for a perfect putter can reach epic proportions. Every golf fan is aware of Arnold Palmer's travails on the greens since his great putting years in the 1960s. Palmer now arrives at golf tournaments with more than a dozen putters in his bag. He has tried more than a thousand different putters over the years. Amateurs, too, have been dogged in their search. While I can certainly empathize if you are one of them, I believe this grab-bag method usually hurts your putting more than it helps.

A proper putter can help your putting game, but you should never lose sight of the need for sound putting mechanics. You must check those mechanics constantly. If you have suddenly developed problems with your putting, it probably is *not* a problem with your putter.

Every putter has a slightly different feel, balance, weight

distribution, location of sweet spot, and grip position relative to the putterface. If you are switching every week, there is no way you can make the subtle adjustments you need to stroke your putts consistently solid.

Putting is my business. It would be easy to simply explain the various advantages of different putters featuring different characteristics. However, I must do more than this. I must also relate *how* these features influence or fit with different stroke patterns and how the resulting putts are affected. What is important is not for you to find out what is the best putter for Arnold Palmer, or for Peter Jacobsen, or for Andy North. You need to be able to determine, to measure, and to understand which putter is best for *you* and *your* stroke. Once you understand how and what to look for, you can make your own choice, and go to the bank with it.

WHAT THE SWEET SPOT IS

The wondrous sweet spot. Is it a point? Is there a sweet-spot area? Can the whole face of the putter be a sweet spot? To understand the concept of sweet spot, we must first define it. The sweet spot is not the center of mass or the center of gravity of the clubhead. The sweet spot is defined technically as the putter's *center of percussion.*

When a putter is swung in a putting stroke, it is actually suspended from a point somewhere between your shoulders. If the putter strikes the ball exactly on its percussion center, the putter slows down its motion around that suspension point, and the golf ball speeds up. There is no twisting or turning of the putterhead; the shock waves sent up the shaft to your hands will be minimized; the impact of the putt feels solid.

In contrast to this, if the putter strikes the ball anywhere away from the center of percussion, not only will the putterhead slow down, it will also turn, twist, wobble, and oscillate to send many more shock waves up the shaft to your hands. The golfer "feels" this mishit as being *not* solid.

According to the laws of physics, the sweet spot is an infinitesimal point. There is no such thing as an "enlarged" sweet spot or a sweet spot that covers the entire face of the putter. Manufacturers or advertisers who promote such a concept are either ignorant or are engaging in "salesmanship." If a ball contacts any putter on a spot other than the true, tiny sweet spot, there is a small vibration, rotation, and loss of energy owing to this mishit. While the energy loss can be minimized by design changes, no design can eliminate it entirely.

SPOTTING THE SWEET SPOT

To locate the sweet spot on your putter, test the putter for lack of rotation or loss of energy when held in a specific position. This must be the exact position you hold the putter in when you putt with it. Often you will see a player hang a putter vertically from his or her fingers and hit the clubface to find the point where no rotation or wobble occurs. This procedure is incorrect; it locates the center of gravity of the putter, not the center of percussion, because when the putter hangs vertically, the entire weight of the shaft and grip are balanced in the center.

In Figure 16.1 I am holding the putter the correct way. That is, the shaft is at approximately a 70-degree angle with the ground, as it is when you putt. As you can see clearly, the weight of almost the entire shaft and grip is balanced on the heel side of the putter. From this position, you can tap the putter with a key or hard object, holding the putter lightly in your fingers so you can feel any rotation or wobble occurring from impact. When you find the point on the putter where there is no wobble, vibration, or shock to your hand, you have located the percussion center, the "real" sweet spot.

FIGURE 16.1:
When looking
for the sweet
spot (center of
percussion) of a
putter, hold the
club with the
shaft at a 70-
degree angle to
the ground, as it
is in the address
position, then
tap to find the
zero wobble
spot.

You see, the exact location of the sweet spot *changes* with the orientation of the putter relative to the ground. If you were to putt with the shaft held nearer to horizontal, for example, as Isao Aoki does, then the sweet spot moves toward the heel because much of the weight of the shaft and grip has been shifted severely in that direction. There is nothing wrong with this, if the golfer now contacts the ball on the new sweet spot. There are, however, some disadvantages to putting like this—namely, if you scuff the putter on the ground, the heel can catch and flip the toe over, causing a severe miss to the left, and the loft angle on the putterface can misalign your putter. However, a good, solid putt can be struck from this position if the putter makes contact on its true sweet spot.

The opposite situation occurs for a player like Payne

Stewart, who putts with his putter sitting on its toe. Payne holds the shaft almost vertically above the head. The sweet spot in this situation is shifted slightly toward the toe, but Payne Stewart strikes it there and is one of the world's best putters doing so. All putters react the same when contacted precisely on their sweet spot. Weight distribution or shape of putter are completely irrelevant to the energy transferred to the golf ball, as long as the ball is hit solidly on the sweet spot.

SHAFT AXIS AND ROTATION AXIS

Impacts not on the sweet spot always cause putterhead rotation, and because golfers hold onto the shaft, the putterheads rotate very nearly around the shaft axis. Therefore, how a putter reacts to a mishit depends not only on how the mass is distributed in the head (which is discussed in the next section), but also on where the shaft is attached to the head.

To determine exactly what happens when balls are mishit by different putters, I ran tests with putters of identical headweights moving at precisely the same speeds. Therefore, all putters had the same energy to transmit to the ball. Figure 16.2 shows the results of two examples from this test, plotted as the distance the ball would roll versus the position of impact on the putterface. If you examine this graph carefully, you will understand why some people like center-shafted putters while others strongly prefer heel-shafted putters.

The energy transferred to the ball when both putters impact on their sweet spots is precisely the same. However, when contact was made toward the toe of both putters, the center-shafted putter reacted better—that is, it transferred more energy to the ball. This means that the center-shafted putter rolled the ball farther and closer to the intended line than did the heel-shafted model. However, the opposite occurred when both putters were struck toward the heel. The

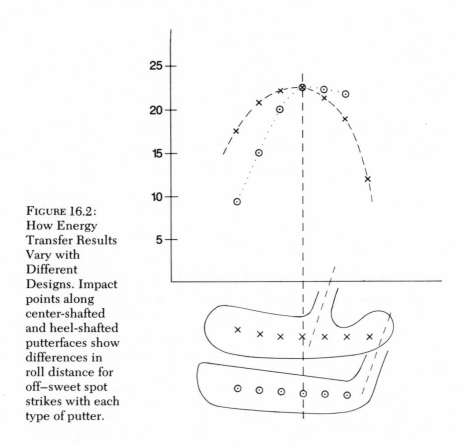

FIGURE 16.2:
How Energy
Transfer Results
Vary with
Different
Designs. Impact
points along
center-shafted
and heel-shafted
putterfaces show
differences in
roll distance for
off–sweet spot
strikes with each
type of putter.

heel-shafted putter reacted better in this case. Simply put, if you tend to mishit puts toward the toe of your putter, you will be better off using a center-shafted putter. If your misses tend to be toward the heel (similar to Trevino, Nicklaus, and Crenshaw), you will probably prefer a heel-shafted putter.

MOMENT OF INERTIA

How much your putterhead turns and dissipates energy on mishits is partly determined by the moment of inertia of your putterhead.

The technical term—moment of inertia—has a very specific meaning in physics. In golf, the term is used as a general measure of a putter's resistance to turning when it is mishit. The greater the moment of inertia, the less the rotation. However, this is not a direct relationship. If the moment of inertia is twice as high, that does not mean the putter rotates only half as much. The amount of rotation and energy dissipation at impact also depend on where the rotational axis of the putter is located and how tightly you hold the putter.

Some advertisers state that if their putter's moment of inertia is twice as high as brand X, then their putter is twice as good as brand X (hinting that you might make twice as many putts with it). Such statements are ridiculous! Performance testing on several putters showed that a putter with a moment of inertia three times higher performed about 10 percent better in terms of the number of putts made. So keep in mind: the higher the moment of inertia, the better the putter feels on mishits, but the less you'll realize you have mishit your putts; your stroke can tend to become sloppier. As with most things in life, there is a trade-off with this feature. The better it feels, the less it tells you about the quality of your stroke. And there are many good players who don't want bad strokes to feel good! They want to know if they make bad strokes, so they can stop making them!

PUTTERHEAD BALANCE

You may have heard a golf professional say that a certain putter is not balanced well, that it is no good. Balance in a putter is not inherently good or bad. Every putter is balanced in some way about its axes, but not all putters are balanced well for you. In fact, very few putters may be balanced properly for the mishit pattern of your stroke.

Both the heel-to-toe and top-to-bottom weight distributions in a putterhead affect the feel of the putter. Most golfers strike the ball approximately $4/10$ inch above the sole of the putter, so if you are among this group, your putter should have its weight evenly distributed above and below this point. In the heel-to-toe direction, most golfers strike the ball toward the toe instead of on the sweet spot. In testing, however, I have found no average impact spot in this direction. Some players contact the ball severely toward the toe, some players strike it toward the heel, and most PGA Tour players stroke the ball almost exactly on the sweet spot. Of course, this heel-to-toe weight distribution influences the moment of inertia and, therefore, strongly affects the feel you judge the putter to have.

There is another weight distribution that affects the balance of a putter, and that is how much weight is in the head compared to weight in the shaft. You may have felt some putters that have weights added inside the shaft. This makes the overall weight of the putter much heavier without making the head weight change to the same degree. In other words, it changes the "feel" of the clubhead, and this may be an advantage to some players (particularly to putters who have the "yips"—see Chapter 19).

The net result of balance is just this: The balance of any putter is good or bad depending only on how the putter reacts to the mishit pattern of your stroke.

WHAT IS FORCE-BALANCING? P. 172

Most putters have been designed according to a system that leads to inaccurate delivery of the clubface through impact. When you make your stroke, you apply a force that is moving in the direction you want the ball to go. For most putter designs, if you swing the putter with an extremely light grip, you'll find that the clubhead fans open substantially in relation to the target line. The greater the stroke force, the more the blade tends to open. Certain putters naturally align themselves open by about 20 degrees; others by as much as 45 degrees to the direction of that force (see Figure 16.3). And there is one popular model that opens by an even greater degree than that!

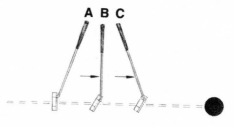

FIGURE 16.3: A non-force-balanced putter (*top*) will tend to open as it moves through impact. The clubface of a force-balanced putter remains perpendicular to the force (square to the target line).

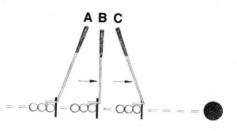

If you are a good putter, you have learned to adjust for this tendency; you have developed a "holding force" to keep your putts from sliding to the right. The longer the putt and the more energy you put into the stroke, the more holding force you must apply. This holding force is the main reason most good putters pull more putts than they push! Under pressure, they are likely to make an overcorrection (and pull the putt) rather than undercorrect and push it. Of course, the error could be either way, but why should any golfer have to make a holding-force correction in the first place, just because of a poorly designed putter?

In a few putters, including my 3-Ball Putter (which I will tell you more about) the club's design allows the putterhead to move down the target line with the face remaining square to the direction of the force. A force-balanced putter, as we call this feature, is self-aligning; you do not need to apply any holding force to keep the blade square to the line! Although it takes a little time to "remove" your usual adjustment, it is simpler in the long run to putt with a force-balanced putter.

P. 170

The Force-Balance Test

Test if a putter is force-balanced by conducting the following experiment. Balance the putter shaft horizontally across your forefinger (see Figure 16.4). With the club in this position, check the clubface. Is it pointing straight up or is it angled to the vertical? Most times, the putterface will angle away; if it points straight up, it is likely to have some force-balancing that helps the clubface stay on line.

VISUAL ALIGNMENT: BIRTH OF THE PELZ PUTTER

Many golfers have great difficulty aiming their putter correctly when they putt. I usually test pro golfers' aim in my test laboratory by setting up a row of twenty-five white golf balls (touching in a line) against one wall, with the center ball brightly colored. I next ask the golfers to stand across the room at various distances from the wall, and aim their putter at the center colored ball. Then by using a laser beam, I measure exactly where they are *really* aiming. Usually it is not even close to the colored ball.

When you consistently aim your putter incorrectly, you develop a subconscious correction in order to make the ball roll where you want it to. The larger the correction, the less consistently you will be able to make the adjustment.

Putting stroke flaws of this nature afflict some of the best players in the world; don't think it is limited to just the middle and high handicappers. Lee Trevino is one who aims left of the hole, then "blocks" his putts to the right. He is a great player, but he is great *in spite of* his putting, not because of it! Given his method, it takes a great athletic performance by Lee to putt well, and certainly he has done so many times. However, if Lee could have putted as well as, say, George

FIGURE 16.4: If you can balance a putter on your fingertip, and if the clubface points straight up, as with the Pelz 3-Ball Putter, it is probably force-balanced.

Archer or Tom Kite, he would have won many more tournaments than he has.

The problem of misalignment can become very complex, because the same player might misalign in a number of different ways. Take Jim Simons. As mentioned earlier, when we first began working together, my measurements showed that on a straight putt of 3 feet, Simons aimed at the left edge of the hole. On a straight 12-footer, Jim aimed perfectly—dead center. But from 30 feet out, he aimed *3½ feet* to the right of the hole! This startling information showed that Simons had to make *different subconscious corrections* for every putt, depending on how far he was from the hole! Under this handicap, Simons, too, needed a tremendous performance to putt well by professional standards.

Obviously, these examples show that aligning the putterface correctly is a big problem for many golfers. And, of course, any putter which has a visual alignment feature that helps you aim better is good. In trying to determine how to help more golfers aim better, several years ago I had an interesting experience.

A FOUR-BALL AIMER

Since I was not an expert on optics, I went to the people nearby who were, at the University of Maryland. I showed them several putters I had made and asked what I could do to help people align them better. We discussed and tested all kinds of visual alignment aids. After several unsuccessful tests, I made an offhand comment that wound up making all the difference in the world: I mentioned that during putting, a golf ball was always sitting in front of the putterface.

My optical experts groaned and asked, "Why didn't you tell us that in the first place?" (I never did ask them what they thought would be sitting there.) They told me human beings tend to relate to, or "see," the outside shapes of things. In other words, what golfers see when they look down at their putter is a round shape sitting in front of a rectangular putterhead. The outline of this shape is a rectangle with a lump at the front. There is no directionality to this shape, and it is difficult to aim, no matter what kind of lines or marks you paint on top of the blade. They then stated, "If you want people to aim more accurately, make the outside shape into something that is very directional, like a line or an arrow."

So I did! I realized I could make a long, white, dotted line appear if I made the putter out of golf balls, and set them in a straight line behind the ball in play. Now I had an even longer line, pointed right at the hole! This turned out to be the best putter to align, ever!

The longer this line of golf balls is, the more accurately you can aim that line. Of course, you can't carry a putter with a head comprising twenty-five golf balls, but you *can* carry a putter with a row of three. And the ball you actually stroke becomes the fourth ball in the alignment system, adding to the length of the line.

I designed my 3-Ball Putter many years before I ever let anyone see it. I was hesitant to bring it out, because I felt I had to establish my own credibility before letting people set eyes on it. Otherwise, they would dismiss it as not a meaningful development. I finally gave a prototype to PGA Tour pros Tom Jenkins and D. A. Weibring, after D. A. had been asking me about what he called a "silly" idea for a putter design (which actually turned out to be force balancing). I wish you could have seen their reactions. At first they thought I was kidding! Then they putted with it and were excited. They said, "Let's run our putter evaluation test" (see Chapter 18), and the rest is history. They both wanted to play the putters on Tour, and in the next three months, D. A. won tournaments all over the world (Japanese Polaroid Cup, Air New Zealand Open) by putting what he termed "the best of my life!" So my conclusion is: If you can aim it better, all other things being equal, you will probably putt better with it!

DOES BEST DESIGN MAKE THE BEST PUTTER?

Now that you understand some of the important features of putter design, you might pose the following questions: "OK, Pelz, I see laying before me a putter that has better alignability and a higher moment of inertia; the putter is force balanced and it is the best possible balance for my putting stroke. Is it the best putter for me? How about the physical fit of this putter? What if it's too short, if the grip's too small? What if the lie or the loft are wrong for me? And besides all this, what if I hate the looks of the putter? Is this really the best putter for me?"

In the next chapter I discuss the fit of putters and how this relates to your putting stroke. Then I will answer those important questions.

17 How Well Does Your Putter Fit You?

It never ceases to amaze me how many golfers play with putters that fit neither their address position nor their stroke mechanics. If you were buying clothes, would you pick a shirt with sleeves an inch too short or pants with cuffs that dragged along the ground? Of course not. You would know immediately that they didn't fit you properly. But it isn't clear to many golfers what constitutes proper "fit" in a putter. In this chapter I examine several important factors to help you get that perfect fit.

THE LONG AND SHORT OF IT

How long a putter should you use? Don't bother to tell me your height, sleeve length, and golf glove size. There's no magic formula to help you find your perfect putter length. But there are ways to determine how the length of the putter affects you.

The length of any golf club—be it putter, iron, or driver —affects how heavy the club *feels* to you. The longer the putter, the heavier the head will feel. This is a sensation you will have as you execute your stroke. The ball doesn't react any differently based on whether your putter is, say, 34 inches rather than 36 inches. The ball only reacts to how heavy the head is and how fast it is moving at impact. The seemingly heavier weight you feel in the putter with the longer shaft is just that—a feeling. Don't worry about it.

However, the length putter you choose can affect the way you position your hands and eyes at address in relation to your body, shoulders, and ball. Assuming you hold your putter near the end of the grip and keep your eyes vertically over the target line, with your back bent at your normal angle, then the longer the putter, the more you need to bend your wrists and elbows. A putter that is too long will also tend to make you set your hands too close into your body, rather than letting them hang vertically below your shoulders, as discussed in Chapter 10.

I favor putters that are slightly shorter than is standard today for most golfers. You will probably find you can let your arms hang down more naturally with a shorter putter and minimize the bend in both the wrists and the elbows. (The smaller the angle between your hands and forearm at address, the less likely you will use substantial wrist motion during the stroke.)

While I prefer to see some players go with a shorter putter, keep one other thought in mind. If you have back problems, as many people do, and it hurts to putt for extensive periods of practice, then you'd be better off using a longer putter. Standing in a more upright fashion may force you to arch your wrists a bit or to assume a slightly unfavorable hand position (hands not directly under the shoulders), but this is still preferable to avoiding practice. One of the best putters in the world, Raymond Floyd, uses a *38-inch* shaft in his putter, 3 to 4 inches longer than normal, for just this reason. Raymond wants to practice for long hours, and he just can't do so with a short putter.

THE EFFECTS OF PUTTER LIE

The lie angle affects your putting in several different ways. First, as we saw in the last chapter, the lie of the putter can "relocate" the sweet spot or center of percussion. If you were to use a putter with a lie that's more upright than it should be for you, the putter will rest on its heel with the toe in the air. The more the toe is off the ground, the more the sweet spot moves toward the heel of the putter. Conversely, if the lie is too flat for you, at address the heel will be off the ground and the sweet spot is effectively moved toward the toe. Either way, you need to make sure to strike your putts solidly.

A second important effect of an improper putter lie is that it can cause you to scuff the ground with whichever end of the blade is lowest. If your putter sits on the heel only, and you happen to scuff the ground slightly before impact, the heel will slow down as it hits the turf and the toe will flip forward. And your putt will roll badly off line to the left! Conversely, players who scuff the toe tend to miss putts in the opposite direction, to the right.

The best solution is to find a putter that sits flat on the ground when you assume your normal address position. The majority of manufacturers design their putters with a 70-degree lie angle as their "standard" (see Figure 17.1). For those who need a more upright lie, look for a 72- or 73-degree lie angle. A 67- or 68-degree lie angle fits those requiring a slightly flatter-than-normal address position. If you find a putter you really like, except that the lie is not right, your golf pro might be able to bend it; or check with the manufacturer. There's a good chance you can get the same model with the lie right for you. And remember, after you have taken the best putting address position for your best stroke mechanics, with your hands vertically under your shoulders and your eyes over the target line, there is *only one* putter lie and length just right for you!

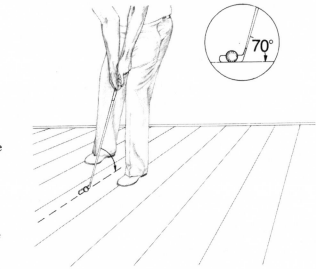

FIGURE 17.1:
The sole of the
putter should be
parallel to the
ground at
address. For a
majority of
golfers, a 70-
degree lie angle
(*inset*) will
provide this.

THERE'S LOFT ON A PUTTER?

Many golfers don't realize that the faces of most putters have
a certain amount of loft. You need a bit of loft to provide a
slightly upward force at impact, to get the ball rolling on top
of the grass (as opposed to driving the ball downward into
the ground and making it start with a bounce). Those aware
of this loft angle should know that it is oftentimes misjudged
because of an error in the way loft is commonly measured.

The true loft angle of a putter is the angle between the
clubface and the shaft (see Figure 17.2). However, many
golfers try to measure the loft *in relation to the bottom of the
putter,* because they assume the sole of the putter should be
flat. It's not. Most manufacturers angle the bottom of the
putter upward, so as you draw the putter back it is less likely
to scuff the ground. If you measure relative to the sole, your
loft angle will appear to be much *greater* than it really is. But

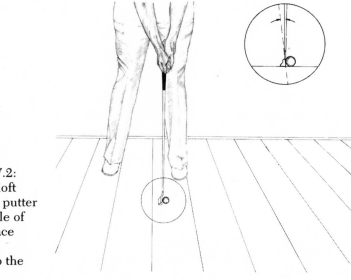

FIGURE 17.2:
The true loft
angle of a putter
is the angle of
the clubface
measured
relative to the
shaft axis.

most important is the effective loft angle of your putter, relative to the ground, at the moment of impact of your putt. The effective loft angle is what determines the direction of the force applied to your putt, and whether your putt bounces or slides and rolls immediately after impact.

A typical example is when the clubface-to-sole angle might indicate 7 degrees and the true loft angle between the face and the shaft is just 2 degrees! In this case the effective loft angle can easily be negative (A) or positive (B), depending on whether you contact the ball with your hands ahead of or behind the ball (see Figure 17.3).

The best effective putter loft angle varies for different grasses in various regions of the country. For the soft bent grasses of the Northeast, a loft angle of only .5 degree to 1 degree is best. Farther south, in Maryland, Virginia, and North Carolina, a loft angle of 2 to 3 degrees is better. In Florida, where bermuda-grass putting surfaces predominate, the best roll is obtained while using 4 to 6 degrees of loft. This same loft range also proves effective in areas along the

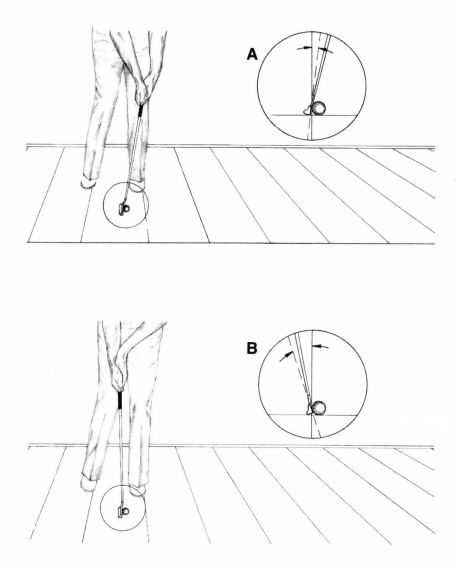

FIGURE 17.3: Effective Loft Angle. Stroking the ball with your hands well ahead (A) reduces the effective loft (*insert A*) at impact. Hands behind the ball at impact (B) adds to effective loft (*insert B*).

West Coast, where greens feature strong-bladed, grainy grasses.

In some areas of the country, there are great variations in the optimum loft angle because the types of grass vary greatly. In Texas, for example, a 5-degree loft works best on the bermuda-grass greens, while on courses with bent-grass greens (of which there are many), a 2-degree loft works better.

Generally, the stronger the grass blades on the greens, the greater the loft needed for optimum results. You want to get your putts rolling *on top of* the grass rather than through it. But don't go overboard with loft and "launch" your putts into the air. Bouncing putts are not good, either. The ideal solution is to use the least amount of loft that will get your putts up and rolling on top of the grass, without getting them airborne.

A "WEIGHTY" QUESTION

Assuming a constant clubhead speed, solid contact, and all other things equal, the heavier the putterhead is, the farther the ball will roll. However, numerous aspects about putter designs are not always equal, and the assumption that heavier putters always roll the ball farther can be *very misleading.*

The heavier the head of the putter, the more the shaft will flex. The more the shaft flexes, the more uncertain the results can be. Some golfers change to a heavier putter and begin to leave putts short (because their shaft kicked at the wrong time and lost energy instead of adding it). Meanwhile, other golfers who move to heavier putters seem to consistently knock their putts past the hole. Be careful and experiment extensively when you change the weight putter you use.

Certain putter weights work better for certain types of golfers. The very nervous putter, someone with a "handsy," manipulative stroke, usually putts better with a heavy-headed putter. The heavier the head (sometimes two to three times heavier than normal), the more difficult it is to manipulate the putterhead. Another possible adjustment for "handsy" putters is to use a very heavy clubshaft. For these players, sometimes I fill the shaft with sand or lead to make the putter more difficult to manipulate.

Both of these weight adjustments can prove very positive in certain cases. However, keep in mind the negative trade-off that can occur when you add weight to the putter: the heavier the putterhead, the slower it must be moving to impart the same amount of energy to the ball. And the slower you move the head, the shorter your stroke and the less tolerance you have to control different speeds for different putts. Simply, the heavier the putterhead, the more difficult it is to achieve good touch for distance. Therefore, if you possess a good, smooth stroke and employ little or no manipulation of the hands, fingers, or wrists, consider a putter that is perhaps a little lighter. You will be able to develop a superior touch and adjust more easily to various green speeds.

PUTTER SHAFTS BEND, TOO

Believe it or not, the shafts of putters actually flex during the putting stroke. On weaker, more flexible-shafted putters, you can actually see deflections, or "bows," in the shaft during the downstroke for a 20-foot putt (see Figure 17.4).

If the shaft is bowing, there will be a shaft "kick" occurring somewhere in your stroke. Because of this kick, some golfers say they love a certain putter and hate another, even though they have identical head designs! The only difference between the two clubs is the degree of flex in the shaft. So what may be good for one player in terms of shaft flex may be bad for another. The question is, does your putter shaft have much kick; and if it does, does it kick at the right time in your stroke for you?

Two of the finest putters I've ever had the privilege to

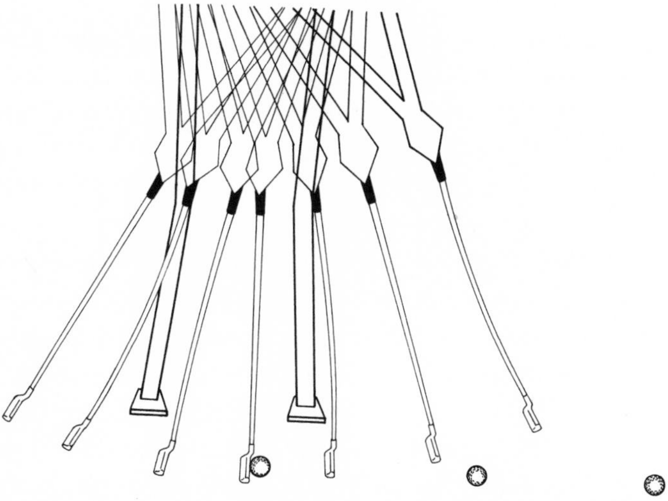

FIGURE 17.4: A flexible shaft may bow backward up to ½ inch during the downstroke, then kick and bow forward during the stroke.

watch, Ben Crenshaw and Deane Beman (former PGA Tour player, now commissioner of the PGA Tour), take exactly opposite views on this flex phenomenon. While Crenshaw uses a very soft, flexible shaft, Beman uses the stiffest he can find. Deane's philosophy is to let him control the putter by himself; he doesn't want any help or uncertainty from anywhere else. Ben, on the other hand, likes the feel of the putterhead and the impact made with a "high-kick" putter shaft. He wants to "know" where the putterhead is and feel its movement throughout the stroke. I can't argue with either of their success; however I usually recommend golfers to consider using the stiffest shaft they feel comfortable with. If you don't have Crenshaw's timing, talent, and smooth stroke, a shaft kick can mean big trouble for you.

WHY BIG GRIPS ARE BEST

The shapes and sizes of putter grips are so varied that they are too numerous to deal with individually. However, there are several general ideas I would like to suggest.

Obviously, the size of your grip should relate to the size of your hands and fingers. If you cannot get a good grip on

the golf club, you can't have a repeatable relationship between your hands and the putterface, as is necessary.

I recommend you try putting with a fairly large grip. The
larger the grip's diameter, the more your hands must be open
to accommodate it. And the more your hands are open,
the more inactive your hands and wrists will be during the
stroke. Particularly, if you are a "handsy" putter and the
problems in your stroke are caused by the use of the muscles
in your hands and wrists, try using a larger grip. You'll find it
much more difficult to manipulate the putter.

The reverse is also true: the smaller the grip, the more
"closed" your hands will be around the club and the more
active your hands will be. While I don't recommend thin
grips for many players, there are some players who feel they
get a little better touch by using them.

With regard to the shape of the grip, I prefer *square-
shaped* grips. I have used such a grip on my own putter for
years; I like it because it helps me keep my palms parallel to
the face of my putter, while also placing my thumbs exactly
parallel to the target line. Also, a square grip has four corners,
which are very easy to "feel." Once you get used to having
your palms on each side of the grip and your thumbs on top,
if you were to hold that putter in any position other than
"square," you would feel the difference immediately!

There are many other popular grip styles, the most predominant being the pistol, paddle and flat top shapes (see
Figure 17.5). Many golfers might prefer one of these shapes
on the basis that they fit into the hands better and are initially
more comfortable. There is nothing wrong with using them,
though the square grip provides more built-in "check-
points."

AN OVERLOOKED ELEMENT—GRIP
ALIGNMENT

Misalignment of the putter grip is one of the *sneakiest, most
devious,* and *least-acknowledged problems* in fitting putters

186

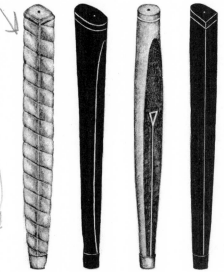

FIGURE 17.5: Grip Types. While I recommend a square putting grip, the pistol, paddle, and flat top styles are very popular, along with many other models.

today. Why do I say this? Because most putter grips are installed by hand, by workers who get paid by the "piece." The more putter grips they install in a day, the more money they earn. And how do they align these grips? How do they make certain they are on perfectly straight? The truth of the matter is that they don't. While certain grip measurement devices exist in most manufacturing plants, workers usually don't use them and the grips are aligned by eye. Most workers try to get the grips on as well as they can, but it is a very inexact process.

Now, I am not knocking these people; they are good workers. However, they are human and the fact is that many (if not most) putter grips are installed crooked!

What happens when you play with a grip that's misaligned? Grip misalignment can be either unimportant, good, or bad, depending on your stroke (see Figure 17.6). Suppose you're putting poorly and decide to try another putter; and just happen to grab one with a grip that's set approximately 1 degree differently from the putter you've been using. This change might make you a little worse *or* a little better, without any change in your stroke!

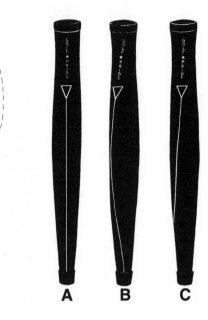

FIGURE 17.6: Misaligned Grips. If the grip is aligned square to the clubface (A), proper alignment of the clubface is much easier. Bowed (B) or twisted (C) grips cause you to "correct" for them, at the same time causing misalignment of the clubface.

A　**B**　**C**

While all golfers have experienced different results when they change putters, very few have attributed the change to a difference in grip alignment. I can assure you that when I change a grip orientation by just 1 degree on a Tour player's putter, I can spot dramatic results. Remember, the better a putter you are, the more important grip alignment is! That's because good players "groove" their hand position for the moment of impact. I've seen excellent putters who, on a whim, decided to change their putter grip. And they never putted as well again. Don't let this happen to you. Be aware that the position of the grip on your putter is extremely important. If you change grips and are puzzled about why you aren't putting as well, this may be the reason.

HOW IMPORTANT ARE LOOKS?

People say that beauty is in the eye of the beholder, and this is certainly true of many aspects of life. Is it also true for putters? Even though a putter may seem beautiful to one golfer while unattractive to another, there are usually very good reasons behind these judgments. The instincts golfers have in deciding what type of putter they like are very meaningful and usually accurate.

Sometimes, there is more to observing something than meets the eye. Have you ever misplaced something? You look all over for it and then a friend walks up and says, "There it is, right there!" "Where?" you ask, puzzled. The friend responds, "Right there in front of you; you're looking right at it!" "Oh yes, you're right," you reply sheepishly. "I was looking at it; I just didn't see it." The same thing can happen when you're searching for the right putter. You may be looking right at what you need, but you just don't recognize it.

Have you ever heard someone say of a certain putter model, "I just hate that putter; I can't line it up at all!" And then someone else, an equally proficient golfer, looks at the same putter and says, "This putter is the best! It's so easy to line up, I just love it." These statements are directly opposed to one another, yet for each individual they are true!

I have done no scientific research to prove this, but I think these feelings are probably based on subconscious recognition of past results, and obviously you'll want to have a good feeling about your putter. Perhaps that little glow of energy, that little spark of affection will help you put your best stroke on your putts. On the other hand, if you don't like the looks of a putter, maybe this will inhibit your ability to execute your best stroke—even if the putter fits you to a tee! Whatever the reason, if the beauty, or appearance, of the putter doesn't fit your emotional or mental attitude, it's not likely you'll ever get your best results from it.

Figure 17.7 illustrates a variety of putter designs. Which one looks like it might be for you? You may already have some idea regarding the model or general style of putter you prefer. Some golfers are "sold" on mallet style putters, for example. Others swear by a certain type of blade. If at this point you're not certain which is right for you, don't worry

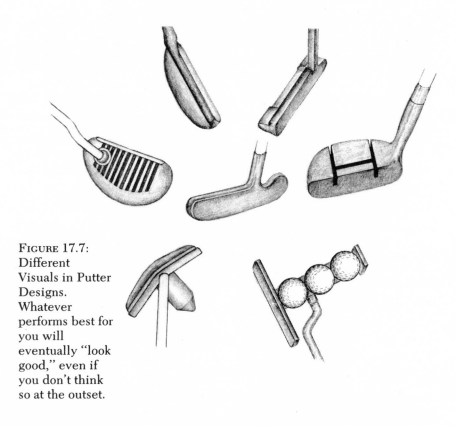

FIGURE 17.7: Different Visuals in Putter Designs. Whatever performs best for you will eventually "look good," even if you don't think so at the outset.

about it. Actually, you are better off keeping an open mind. Don't put limits on your chances of finding what works best for you.

"FEEL" CAN BE AN ILLUSION

I started my research into putting believing that feel is determined by the transmission of shock from the impact of the club with the ball, a shock which moves up the shaft into the hands. Well, feel is partly that. But, surprisingly, another part of feel is actually the *sound* the putter makes when it strikes the ball. It's amazing how golfers relate sound to the results of a particular shot, whether it is a putt or a drive. Have you ever played on a course located next to an airport? If you have, you may have hit a shot just at the moment a plane was passing overhead and you couldn't hear any sound at impact. When you can't hear any sound at impact, the *feel* seems terrible too, even when you have made a good swing or stroked a good putt.

You may like a steel putterface, the next person might like brass, the next, aluminum. In reality it may be the *sound* that you like. So don't judge a putter solely by the feel at impact. It's just too subjective.

IS IT POPULAR?

I see it happen so often. An amateur golfer "decides" he really likes a certain style of putter for a reason that has nothing to do with how it rolls the ball or how he or she putts with it. He simply starts to "like" whatever putter his favorite Tour pro has turned to. After all, if Jack Nicklaus or Tom Watson or Raymond Floyd or Tom Kite uses a certain putter, it's good enough for him!

It's easy to jump on the bandwagon and go with whatever your favorite pro is using. It might even give your confidence a shot in the arm. For a while. Eventually, though, the euphoria wears off, and if that particular model doesn't suit your stroke, you won't hole as many putts as you should. So don't let an advertising campaign or a Tour pro's endorsement make that decision for you.

Ultimately, a golf ball on a green doesn't react to the popularity, the look, or the feel of the putter you select. The ball responds only to the path, the clubface angle, the impact point, and the energy transmitted by the putterface at the moment of impact. And you know that the look and feel, the physical fit, loft, lie, length, moment of inertia, and shaft axis all affect the player's ability to execute the stroke to some degree. They are all of significance in your final putter choice. So if by now you're slightly confused and not sure what kind of putter you even like the look of, I'll show you how to find the right putter in the next chapter.

18 Performance: The Ultimate Test in Choosing a Putter

With all you have read about putters in the last two chapters, you might be wondering whether the putter you're currently using is effective, given your putting style. And well you should! The putter is the least uniform club in the bag. Your so-called standard putter may vary in length from 33 to 36 inches. The clubhead design may be any one of hundreds of different shapes. And the club's loft angle, weight, moment of inertia, shaft location, balance, look, and feel can be of almost infinite variety.

As to materials, the putter head may be constructed of steel, brass, aluminum, wood, zinc, lead, plastic, graphite, and who knows what else! And, of course, your putter may come with alignment aids designed to help you set up properly in relation to your target line. So even though you may like your putter and feel "comfortable"' with it (after using it for a number of years), you may still want to consider whether your putter is really the best one for you.

When all is said and done, what is most important about your putter is how it performs in concert with *your* putting stroke. Does it help you get the ball into the hole or doesn't it? You must take a very pragmatic outlook at this stage.

When you find a putter that helps you make more putts, use it! *Don't* be overly concerned with how it looks, how it feels, or how it sounds. Believe me, the best "feeling" of all is picking the ball out of the hole after your first putt!

WHAT ABOUT PHYSICS, PHYSICAL FIT, AND LOOKS?

When I say performance is all that counts, you might think at first that I am contradicting myself. Does this mean the factors discussed in the last two chapters don't really matter? No. *All* these factors matter. Each fit should be evaluated carefully and determined the best possible for you. Then when you have found one or more putters that appear to be right, it is time to perform some objective testing. Determining the overall performance of a particular putter is really not that difficult.

THE TOUR PROFESSIONAL PERFORMANCE TEST

I use this performance test with PGA Tour professionals. But even if you're not a pro, you still should be able to apply this test to your own putting game.

This is a contest between two putters, usually the model you currently use and a new putter you think might work better. There are ten steps, as follows:

1. Set up a test sequence on your practice putting green, consisting of ten putts varying in length from 3 to 30 feet, in 3-foot increments. The putts should fan out on a level area so all putts will roll relatively straight (see Figure 18.1 for the actual configuration of the test area).
2. Mark each spot by placing a tee in the green.
3. The area within your stance positions and footprints, covered by dashed lines in Figure 18.1, should not be walked on during the test.

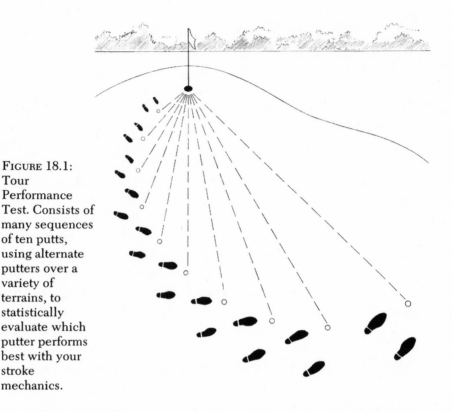

FIGURE 18.1:
Tour
Performance
Test. Consists of
many sequences
of ten putts,
using alternate
putters over a
variety of
terrains, to
statistically
evaluate which
putter performs
best with your
stroke
mechanics.

4. Place a golf ball at each of the ten spots you've marked. With Putter A, hit each putt in sequence, starting with the 3-foot putt and working your way out and around to the 30-foot putt. No second chances allowed! Look over each putt and read each putt prior to stroking. Record how many of the putts you sink. (You may need to recruit a volunteer to keep score during the test. It's important that you keep your mind on putting, not on keeping score. You must think only about making putts, not about which putter is going to "win" the contest!)

5. Next, hit each putt with Putter B. As always in this test, you get one chance only with each putt.

6. Repeat the ten-putt sequence with Putter B, then repeat it again with Putter A. Record all data on the "make percentage" with each putter. For example, the results may be as follows: Putter A, two of ten; Putter B, three

of ten; Putter B, three of ten; Putter A, two of ten. This completes the straight-putt sequence.

7. Set up and execute four more identical ten-putt sequences, except this time on uphill, then downhill, then left-to-right breaking, and finally right-to-left breaking putts. Again, each sequence should be ten putts fanned out in this same shape, as shown in Figure 18.1. (This configuration allows you to hit all putts without stepping in the line of any other putt. If you're left-handed, you must reverse the direction of the fan.)

8. Reverse the order in which you use Putter A and Putter B for each sequence. For example, the order for the straight putt was A-B-B-A. For the uphill segment, it's B-A-A-B. The downhill segment is once again A-B-B-A. The left-to-right sequence is B-A-A-B, and the right-to-left group is A-B-B-A.

9. After you've followed this cycle once, repeat the entire test on another day. When you repeat it, use the opposite putter first within each sequence. (If you used Putter A first the previous time for that sequence, use Putter B first this time.)

10. Tabulate the results. In each sequence you'll have hit 20 putts with each putter. After the first round, you'll have totaled 200 putts, 100 with each putter. After completing the second round, at the end of the test you'll have putted 200 putts with each putter for a total of 400 putts. (Incidentally, your test results will be more accurate if you conduct the test early in the morning, right after the greens have been cut. The earlier the test, the fewer footprints.)

IS THE TEST WORTH IT?

Granted, testing putters in this manner takes quite a while. Normally you can set up and complete one cycle (200 putts) in about an hour. Then you should stop and do something else, perhaps hit balls or go play nine holes. Don't try to putt for so long that you become stale and aren't giving each putt your best. If you can spend an hour on two different days, you can complete the entire test comparison.

Once you've completed this test and tabulated the results, you'll *know* which putter performs better for you! There won't be any question in your mind. And besides giving you this information, the test is a great way to practice.

THE PRACTICE GREEN PERFORMANCE TEST

Here's a modified version of the Tour Pro test, one you can accomplish in a single session.

Naturally, the statistics you'll derive from this test aren't infallible. You can't have quite as high a confidence factor in the results. But if there is a strong difference in performance between the two putters you're testing, it should become evident. Here are the steps to follow:

1. Set up a putting test area as shown in Figure 18.2. It is similar to the previous test, but in this one use just five balls instead of ten. Set them at spots marked off at 3, 9, 15, 21, and 27 feet from the cup.
2. Putt each sequence with Putter A and then Putter B. Then reverse putters so that you have the A-B-B-A sequence, as in the first test. At this point, you'll have stroked ten putts with each putter. Record the number sunk using each putter.
3. Set up the same five putt sequences as used in the Tour Pro test. In addition to the straight flat sequence, arrange one sequence that's uphill, one that's downhill, one that's left-to-right, and one that's right-to-left. Repeat the same putting process for each.
4. Total your "make" percentage for all five sequences for each putter. You'll have stroked 50 putts with each putter, a total of 100 putts.

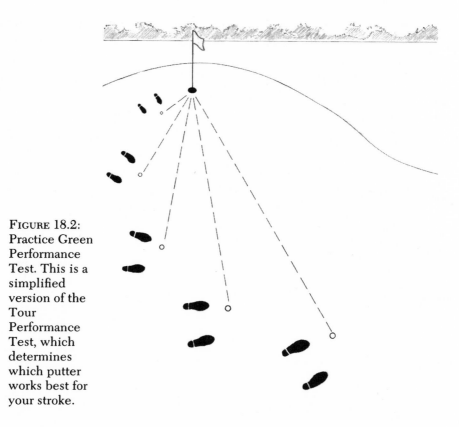

FIGURE 18.2:
Practice Green
Performance
Test. This is a
simplified
version of the
Tour
Performance
Test, which
determines
which putter
works best for
your stroke.

You can complete the Practice Green Performance Test in about thirty minutes and, again, it is very good practice. As with the Tour Pro test, it's best to have a scorekeeper so you won't be distracted from the task at hand by thinking about which putter is "winning."

With this shorter test, you're doing it all in one session. Therefore, you won't be able to "average out" the day-to-day variables in your putting stroke and in the green conditions and their influences. However, if you sink a significantly higher number with one putter than the other, you ought to want to use that putter. No matter what you thought before!

The Practice Green Performance Test is easy enough and short enough to run. Consider performing it several times each golf season. If your putter "wins" every time over a series of comparisons you should begin to develop a sense of confidence that it is very good for you, given your stroke pattern.

A TOTAL FIT

If you've attended to all my suggestions about choosing the best putter, you'll enjoy both the scoring improvement the club will provide, and you'll have the satisfaction of knowing you've gone the "extra mile" that others haven't. You *deserve* to make more putts! And you will!

PART V: The Mental Side of Putting

19 You Can Cure the Dreaded Yips

If you're confident, competent, and have absolutely no fear of short putts, you can turn merrily to the next chapter. You don't have to worry about the "yips," that score-ruining phenomenon that causes a player to "jerk" the stroke on very short putts and miss them terribly.

In fact, if you're a "nonyipper," you might be a little annoyed that there *is* a chapter on this subject. Like shanking in the full swing, yips are something golfers don't like to hear about in the first place. Why bring them up? Why even mention the problem?

Well, for the golfer who has known the mental agony that the yips can inflict, this is the most important chapter in the book. Over the years, I have witnessed some incredible cases of the yips. I have seen a player with the yips who can make 100 consecutive beautiful practice strokes, then step up to a 1-foot putt and yip it so badly that it never touches the hole. I've seen good golfers miss putts from 3 inches! One player who had been a one-handicapper had the yips so badly he claimed it ruined not only his golf game but his business, his marriage, his entire life!

Yes, the yips can be a dire predicament, but let's get one thing straight: they are curable! The yips aren't some kind of voodoo or curse. Rather, yips are caused by a slow-developing deterioration of a player's confidence, which in turn is always rooted in unsound stroke mechanics. Curing the yips takes hard work and dedication, but they *have* been cured many times. You can cure them, too.

WHAT HAPPENS WHEN YOU YIP?

My contact with the yip phenomenon started when an old friend of mine went on the Tour, was very successful in his first year, and had the potential to become a great player. Then he got the yips. He adopted the croquet-style putting stroke (later popularized by Sam Snead) in an attempt to overcome the yips, which worked for a time. But then the U.S. Golf Association outlawed this style, and he never got all the way back to becoming the player he could have been.

During his career, this friend studied the yips and eventually spoke to neurosurgeons about the problem. Their explanation of what causes the yips is fascinating.

There is a natural reaction in the human brain to situations of tremendous stress, which neurosurgeons refer to as a "fail-safe shutdown." People who survive terrible accidents have been studied and asked afterward what they recall about the accident itself. For example, a person driving his car had a head-on collision with a truck. As the inevitability of the crash became apparent, the victim drank in virtually every possible detail, as if everything were happening in slow motion. His awareness was amazing. He remembered exactly what the grill of the oncoming truck looked like—the bugs that were stuck in the grill, the crack in the windshield, the way the ornament on top of the grill was turned sideways. He remembered that the truck driver was chewing tobacco and that his eyes looked as big as pie plates as he too realized the inevitability of the crash.

The key point about the recollections of people in such terrible accidents is that they *don't remember the actual im-*

pact! They may have been severely injured and battered, yet when they remember every detail leading up to the crash, they cannot remember the crash itself.

The reason, neurosurgeons explain, is that in situations like this, the fail-safe shutdown goes into effect. The brain senses the heart can't stand the shock of what's about to happen (heart attacks tend to occur when the heart rate exceeds about 200 beats per minute), so it shuts off an instant before disaster strikes. In other words, people just pass out! They can't remember it, because they never saw it!

We all know people who faint at the sight of blood. It doesn't have to be their own, but the sight of blood connotes a strong image of danger to them and they pass out. Of course, others don't react this way. Different people have different thresholds at which the fail-safe mechanism gets triggered.

How do these catastrophes relate to the golfer suffering from the yips? Let's look at how a yip actually develops.

The phenomenon that leads to the yips begins in a player's mind long before it shows up in his or her stroke. The player may have been a respectable or a very good putter for a long time. But then he goes through a period in which he notices he's missing more short putts than usual. He begins to worry about it. In this "preyip" stage, before the player actually has a jerk in his stroke, the misses occur because of one or more technical flaws in the stroke, such as we've already studied.

After a while, the player begins getting more and more negative and fearful over the short ones. (Actually this phenomenon can occur on *any* putt or, really, any shot. I've seen golfers get the yips on chip shots so badly that they shank the ball or stub the ground behind the ball and whiff it completely. It happens most often on short putts because that's where the pressure and fear of missing is greatest.) Starting to *believe* you're going to miss putts is the first phase leading to the yips. The player's subconscious starts talking every time he has a short putt: "I'm probably going to miss the darn thing." Pretty soon it becomes: "I *know* I'm going to miss. I wish I could putt better, I wish I could make myself make it."

In time, golfers get so fearful about missing short putts that the fail-safe mechanism normally associated with great danger kicks into action. For a split second during the stroke, the player actually passes out!

Now the golfer's period of unconsciousness (which is the actual "yip") lasts only about 1/1000 of a second! Usually, this period occurs *just before impact.* The jerk of the putter which causes the player to contact the ball so erratically is actually the *recovery* from the yip. The golfer comes out of that tiny instant of unconsciousness just the way you might come out of a short nap: with a slight jump or a start. The small muscles of the hands react most strongly and contract to catch the putter which they just released for 1/1000 of a second.

This explanation of the yips makes a great deal of sense and falls in line with everything I've seen having to do with the yips. So if you play with someone who's experiencing the yips, have compassion. Don't admonish the person to "get hold" of him or herself. That will only make the fear worse. The person can't control where the ball goes anyway, because he or she is unconscious when it happens!

A PROFILE OF THE YIPPER

There have been a number of famous players who've suffered from the yips, and the affliction certainly isn't limited to lesser golfers. The great Ben Hogan had them.

Hogan, as you know, may have been the most dedicated golfer of all time. But late in his career his putting stroke wasn't very good and, consequently, he wasn't holing many putts. Naturally, as he continued to putt poorly, Hogan's fear of missing increased. He also faced added pressure because so many people watching him were calling him the greatest golfer of his time, then seeing him miss all those easy putts. So the problem grew in greater proportions. Hogan's yips got so bad that instead of yipping as his putter came into contact with the ball, he yipped before he even took it back! At the end of his playing career, he couldn't make the club move away from the ball. It was as if his brain was saying, "Ben, I'm not going to let you take it back because if you do, then you'll come forward and when you come forward, I know you'll miss the putt!" That's a super-severe yip, the ultimate case.

Now there haven't been many people who've played the game who were brighter, more studious, more sincere, and more willing to practice than Ben Hogan. This is the profile of the golfer who is the most likely candidate to get the yips. First you must be intelligent enough to perceive that you're missing more than your share of putts. The golfer who is unaware of how well or poorly he putts will never get the yips. Also, you must care enough about your game to worry about your inability to solve your putting problems. Again, golfers who don't care never get the yips! And, finally, you must practice a lot, making many thousands of strokes, to convince yourself (or more accurately your subconscious) that you're probably going to miss the next putt.

So the prerequisites for the yips are intelligence, caring, and a willingness to work. Funny, isn't it, that those are also three of the prerequisites for greatness?

So don't ridicule your golfing friend who has the yips the next time you see him or her. Because if that friend of yours, who has intelligence, sincerity, and is willing to work, subsequently conquers the yips, he or she just may beat you into the ground for the rest of your golfing career!

A CASE AGAINST BAD NERVES

The yips are constantly attributed to bad nerves, old age, or both. I believe these rationalizations are false. When a player gets the yips, he reasons, "My nerves are no good" because he doesn't know what else to say. Well, you've only got one set of nerves that runs through your body. If they are reacting properly to your other golf movements but seem to betray you on the short putts, then it is your *brain* that's causing the problem, not your nerves!

Let me give you an example. Arnold Palmer was a great putter in the later 1950s through the mid-'60s when he was winning so many tournaments. He made putts from all distances and also sank a good percentage of his short ones. Eventually, though, Palmer got into some bad habits regarding his fundamentals and his putting performance dropped off a bit. At that point, he tried to work on his putting, but he made the fatal mistake that so many golfers do; he *assumed* he knew what he was doing wrong. He made some changes, but they weren't the right ones. Things got worse, so he made even more changes. It didn't take long before it became impossible for "Arnie" to get back to the stroke he used at his best. He couldn't remember what he used to do. He continued to slowly go downhill from there and concluded that his "putting nerves" were no longer any good.

If Arnold Palmer's nerves were no good, how could he still hit the fine drives, iron shots, bunker shots, and chips that he does on the Senior Tour? The truth is, his nerves were fine; his putting stroke and brain just needed a little work, in that order. (Don't bet against him, with his talent and determination, I believe he may be back yet!)

ARE THERE "AGE" YIPS OR "COURAGE" YIPS?

The yips have nothing to do with old age per se, either. Look at Bernhard Langer (see Figure 19.1). Langer suffered a severe and well-documented case of the yips at age nineteen! However, Langer was very dedicated. He made improvements in his stroke fundamentals and he regained his confi-

FIGURE 19.1: Bernhard Langer,
one of the world's top players,
overcame a siege of the yips early
in his career.

dence as well as retrained his brain. Now he can play and putt with anybody in the world and, in fact, at times I think he is *the best* in the world.

True, golfers who have the yips usually are older rather than younger. The reason isn't age itself or the loss of nerves, however. It's simply that a golfer usually has to have played for a long time, endured poor mechanics, and many missed putts before that fear of missing becomes so great it takes hold in the mind. The yips don't happen overnight. It takes many years of bad practice before they take over, thus the tendency for older golfers to develop them.

I'm convinced that devil-may-care individuals will never be victimized by the yips. They simply don't have much fear of the consequences. If they have a bad putting round, they shrug it off. They never feel so terrorized that their brain shuts down, so they can't get a yip as a reaction.

Some people associate an inability to make short putts

with a lack of "courage" or "guts." I disagree with this entirely. I really admire yippers, as well as have great empathy for them. They've practiced hard, they've cared, and they are smart enough to know they've got a problem. They just didn't have the feedback or the knowledge of how to solve their putting-stroke problems when they needed it.

Curing the yips takes time and educated effort. But before explaining the course of action, let me give the yippers of the world a thought to keep them going: from the cases I have seen, the cured yipper winds up being a whale of a putter! This person has been through a difficult battle and conquered it. He or she is as tough in the clutch as they come.

TO SOLVE THE YIPS

Step 1: Remove the Hole. The first step to curing the yips is to *remove the hole* you're aiming at. The overwhelming fear which causes the yip is that of missing the hole. When a golfer makes a practice stroke there is no fear. How can you "miss" a practice stroke? There's no target, nothing to miss, nothing to fear. So whenever you work on your own stroke, place an object a couple of feet down the target line so the ball is deflected almost immediately.

Step 2: Improve the Stroke. Find the problems in your stroke mechanics that are causing you to miss putts, then improve these mechanics through constant repetition of the correct movement. This is an instance in which you absolutely *must* make a correct analysis of the problem, and using the proper feedback device is essential (read Chapters 6 to 12 very carefully).

There are no shortcuts. You *must* know your stroke factors are being executed correctly. You have to improve the stroke that caused you to develop the yips in the first place. If you don't improve your stroke (if you merely practice the same things you've always done except you don't putt to a hole) and you hope you get your confidence back, you are just fooling yourself. The brain is too smart to get tricked that easily. As soon as you go back to putting at the hole, if you have the same faulty stroke as before, you're going to miss too many putts, and get the yips again. Identify the stroke problems and fix them.

Step 3: Repeat the Good Stroke. After you've isolated the mechanical problems and learned how to correct them, then comes the tedious, absolutely essential part of curing the yips. You need to make 20,000 "good" strokes with your new technique (still without pressure of putting to a hole) to build muscle memory.

Right now I'm sure you're saying, "20,000 strokes! That's an awful lot. Can't I do it with 10,000 strokes or maybe 5,000?" No, you can't. Research in behavior modification has convinced me that long-term muscle memory *starts* to set in when you've repeated a movement 10,000 times. You need 20,000 repetitions to reach the point at which the new stroke is firmly in place. Until then, your old stroke will try to creep back in. You have to make enough good strokes so that your new "good" feedback overwhelms the old "bad" feedback in your mental computer—until you get to the point at which your muscles never call up your bad stroke again.

Years ago, while I was rebuilding my own stroke, I worked for thirty minutes every night, during which time I made about 100 strokes. At the end of each session I was always better than when I started, but the next day I was back to my old stroke again. That's because until I had made enough good strokes, my muscles kept referring to the many thousands of bad strokes I had grooved back at Indiana University.

So you need to make 20,000 *proper* strokes to get rid of that yip stroke. Let me break that down into a practice regimen that's a little less intimidating:

Number of evenings of practice per week	5
Time per session (minutes)	30
Number of successful strokes per session	100
Number of strokes per week	500
Number of weeks to ingrain new stroke	40

At this pace it will take forty weeks (about nine months) to replace your yip-causing stroke with a sound one. You'll gain on it a little every day with this very realistic timetable. Of course, you can speed up if you're willing to make 200 practice strokes per night, and/or practice seven days a week, but I don't recommend this. You might be overwhelmed. If this timetable is too stringent, cut back on it a little. It's better to practice for a shorter time each evening (but make it quality time) than to get tired and practice haphazardly.

By the way, a golfer fighting the yips should *not* stay completely away from the course while working on the stroke. Everybody wants to get out on the course once in a while (although if you have the yips you might not want to be out there much anyway!). If you do play, realize that you're not ready to play for "score." Concentrate *only* on the mechanics of your stroke. Read and line up the putt, then think about the stroke and forget about the results (as well as your score). Otherwise, you'll just add to the yip feedback. Play as relaxed as you can during this period and don't worry about your successes and failures if you play in tournament competition.

MENTAL TOUGHNESS: THE FINAL INGREDIENT

Believe it or not, the hardest part of yip therapy isn't "grooving the fix." The most difficult part comes *after* you've accomplished that, when you go back to the course and start competing in earnest again. Now you've got a new stroke, but you're taking it "into the heat" for the first time. You will probably *still* yip for a while! It's not because your stroke is no good. It's because your subconscious is still in the habit of yipping. It does not trust your new stroke yet, and you will yip until you prove you can putt up to your standards.

During this time, tremendous disappointment can set in. Understand the situation and believe in yourself and what you are doing. You've got to continue using your new stroke, to keep showing your brain that this stroke really rolls the ball nicely. Soon you'll have a breakthrough. You'll sink a short one you had previously been yipping, and it will seem very matter-of-fact. Your brain will say to itself as you walk off the green, "Hey, that wasn't much of a problem. You can do that almost every time."

IT REALLY WORKS

A few years ago I worked with a PGA Tour player who had a severe case of the yips. He worked diligently to rebuild his stroke as I have outlined above, and then afterwards, it took him another three months before he played a complete 72-hole tournament without yipping a putt. But he hasn't yipped since.

If you have been battling the yips unsuccessfully, you now know what you need to do. And if you've never had the yips, perhaps you'll benefit from this discussion also. You know the importance of constantly checking your setup and stroke so you can catch any bad habits before they get too well established and can cause problems.

20 The Role the Mind Plays

Golfers do not make the ball move with their mind. I have tried this. I have set the ball many times on the edge of the hole and challenged people to move the ball into the hole with their minds. Just ⅛ inch. Move the ball and make that putt without striking it with the putter. I have not yet seen anyone do this.

However, don't think that I am saying the mental side of putting is not important. The mind controls the body, the body controls the putter, and the putter controls the golf ball. Therefore, the mind is integral in starting the ball on its proper line at its proper speed. But after impact I believe God and the greens are in control of the situation.

The mind cannot make putts for you, but believe me, it can stop you from making putts in a New York minute. If the mind is not in concert with what the body is doing, if the mind has fear or uncertainty, if the mind is distracted and subconsciously against what you are about to do, your body will not move right.

VISUALIZATION

You have to use your mind in order to understand putting. But you can also use your mind to create positive images that will help you sink putts.

Stand behind your next putt and visualize your ball rolling along an imaginary line into the hole. If the ball line starts out initially along the target line, which is, say, 2 inches outside the left edge of the cup, then as it nears the hole and slows it gradually bends, curves, and rolls right into the center of the cup; it is a perfect putt. If you can see this ball rolling in your mind's eye, then imagine the line along which the ball rolls. Remove the ball and try to imagine the line. Now reverse the process. If you see the line in your mind's eye, imagine a ball rolling at a speed along that line. As you perform these mental gymnastics you are, in essence, exercising your mental muscles just as surely as you are exercising your body when you do push-ups, sit-ups, or jog. The more vividly you can imagine these events—the clearer the image is in your mind's eye—the better your body can reproduce these events in real life.

Children can and do imitate athletes they see perform. I believe this is one of the major reasons for the dramatically improved athletic accomplishments in every sport in recent years. As young minds watch the world's greatest athletes perform, they can learn and create vivid images of how things should be done. Then their bodies can better reproduce these events.

"IMAGINE" WINNING

Can you see yourself walking to the presentation, standing in front of the crowd, and accepting the winner's trophy? If you can imagine this chain of events, then run the tape backwards in your mind and imagine yourself reacting to your winning putt. How would you look? How would you behave? Think about this and try to see it. Can you actually see yourself stroking the winning putt? What does that stroke look like? Did you go through your preshot routine exactly as you have 20,000 times in practice? Of course you did. The only way you could make that winning putt is by putting your best stroke on it. And your best stroke only proceeds by following your best preshot routine. What is your best preshot routine? It's the same routine you've used 20,000 times in your den, office, or hotel room, in your Putting Track using the Teacher Putter.

If you stroke that winning putt using your normal routine and the stroke that always follows, then you've done the best you can do. That is the way you will look when you win. If you can imagine that, if you can make that image vivid, if you can create a movie in your mind of what it will look like, what it will feel like, what it will be like, then your chances of actually achieving such an event will be greatly enhanced.

If Jack Nicklaus had an edge over the rest of the golfers that he has played against in his lifetime, it may have been the result of his ability to create this image more vividly than the rest of us. He is a special golfer, but he didn't strike the ball better than the rest of us. I think he imagined what he was about to do better than we did.

DON'T THINK . . . DO

You don't have to be a Rhodes scholar to putt well. You certainly don't need to have studied the physics of putting as I have done for twenty years. All you need to do is develop good habits and a reliable automatic stroke. And that will allow you to putt like the pros. Basketball players don't really think about the mechanics of their jump shot or their dribble during the game. They just do it. Tennis players don't really think about the execution of a backhand during the match, they just do it. Now don't get me wrong, athletes do have key thoughts that help them perform better. Sometimes the key thoughts work, sometimes they don't, and the reason this is true is that the key thought itself is not what matters. It's not that you think about the mechanical motions you make, it's that you focus your mind on something so your subconscious mind and body can get on with the business at hand.

The key to thinking during performance is to not do it. If you have trained your body in a routine fashion over a substantial period of time, the body will follow the pre-planned routine. Systems in their subconscious control mode *love* to have routine. Humans love to form habits. And we are all "creatures of habit" in golf. If you practice properly, if you use the practice routines suggested in the last few chapters, and if you do them while religiously using your preshot routine, you will form the proper habits. Then to perform well when the heat is on, all you have to do is let it happen.

The task of your mind is to give your body the guidance of a bright, vivid, visual image, and then let it rip. Get "into" your preshot routine and go, while the image is strong. Create the image and go. Don't think, do!

21 Are You Willing to Get Worse—Before You Get Better?

I've covered a lot of ground regarding the development of your putting game. You've learned about the factors in the playing surface that can keep even a machine from making every putt. You've learned the three basics of good stroke mechanics, how you can improve your reading of the greens, how to prepare to execute each stroke, how to pick the right putter, and how to practice to acquire a better touch. Technically, you know enough to become a fine putter, maybe even a great one!

There are only two things that can keep you from achieving your goals on the greens: your willingness to work intelligently and your ability to be patient with regard to your results.

THE PUTTING STROKE IS SIMPLER THAN A WALK IN THE PARK

While acquiring an effective putting stroke may take a significant amount of time, once learned, the stroke itself is physically simple to execute. A long time ago, when I decided to take on the task of learning everything I could about putting, I started studying the motions of the human body. My intent was to find out just how difficult it is to make a putting stroke.

After comparing the motions required for walking with those used for putting, I concluded that it's about 100 times more difficult to *walk* than it is to putt! Walking requires more coordination, more muscle control, more strength, more balance, and more motion of small bones and muscles. Yet walking is not difficult. You never think about it; you've been walking ever since you were a little over a year old.

Think about the way babies learn to walk. They crawl over to their mother, pull themselves up to their mother's knee, then look across the room at their father. With a big grin, they take one step toward their dad and fall. Then they crawl back to their mother, pull themselves up again, take one or two steps, and fall again. This goes on for several days. The key is that every time children make a wrong move, they fall! Falling supplies them with *immediate, accurate, reliable feedback.* And babies learn rapidly. After a week or so, they can walk across the room; shortly after that, they are running everywhere!

When a one-year-old gets immediate, accurate, reliable feedback, he or she can learn a relatively difficult maneuver easily. By comparison, look at how many grown men and women have trouble executing the much simpler motion, the putting stroke. This indicates not that putting is difficult, but rather that adults lack the feedback to learn to do it properly.

The putting stroke is the simplest swing in golf. It doesn't require strength, agility, coordination, flexibility, or timing. Any "little old lady" is physically capable of knocking a ball all the way across a putting green and into the hole. But to do it consistently well requires knowledge, experience, touch, and precision. All these skills can be learned. I have yet to see a player work with the system described in this book for a reasonable amount of time and not improve his or her putting.

WHY REGRESSION CAN PRECEDE IMPROVEMENT

My system for improving your putting requires two things: dedication and patience. You cannot perfect your putting stroke overnight. The more changes you need to make, the longer it will take to rid yourself of the compensating factors that exist in your current stroke. There are no shortcuts; I can't tell you anything today that will guarantee you a good putting round tomorrow. But if you work with this system for the necessary time and then keep your improved stroke in tune, I can promise you *better putting for the rest of your golfing life*.

All the teaching devices I've described (Teacher Alignment Computer, Putting Track, and Teacher Putter) are designed to train you to *subconsciously* control the mechanics of your stroke (path, face angle, and impact point). In using them or similar tools, you'll get honest feedback you have never had before. At first you must give conscious thought as to why your stroke keeps banging the rails of the track or why your putts keep hitting the prongs of the Teacher Putter. Stay with it. When you've practiced enough, your subconscious system will take over.

During the period when you are improving your stroke, you must accept a relatively short time period during which your results *may* regress. Notice I didn't say your *stroke* may regress, just your putting results. For example, suppose you are trying to square up your stroke path, which was formerly outside to inside, but you still are contacting the ball with an open blade. Assuming your path is becoming more square and you are lining up correctly, for a while you will miss putts to the right. You've removed one of your stroke flaws (bad path), and that's certainly a step toward an improved stroke! But the removal of one flaw doesn't help you sink putts, until you have also removed the other compensations, too.

It takes a certain open-mindedness to allow yourself to

accept "worse" results while you are consciously adjusting your mechanics. Remember that in reality you are *not* getting "worse"; you are simply correcting different flaws, at separate rates. When you have corrected them all, you will sink more putts. It may not be obvious that you're improving, and you may have to pay off a few bets in the interim, but you'll know you're improving. Keep your chin up! The best players on the PGA Tour willingly go through these stages; they know the day will come when the sacrifice will pay off handsomely.

As your stroke mechanics improve you'll find you can execute them successfully without as much conscious thought. You'll even get to the point at which you can execute your stroke fundamentals consistently while watching television, talking to someone, or listening to music. In fact, I have a speaker phone hookup that lets me conduct telephone conversations while I practice my stroke.

You will find that as you improve your mechanics, you will gradually get bored by them because there will be an absence of negative feedback; you aren't any longer hitting the rails with your stroke or knocking the prongs guarding the sweet spot on the blade, for example. This is why it's so helpful to have *adjustable* feedback devices, so you can tighten these stroke governors to increase the "degree of difficulty" as you improve.

PICK YOUR PRACTICE REGIMEN

The more intelligently you practice, the sooner you will see improvement. Remember that when you are reconstructing your stroke, or rebuilding any muscular movement, it takes at least 10,000 successful repetitions before your new muscle memory *begins* to overcome (20,000 to replace) the muscle memory of your old stroke. It also takes some time (which varies from individual to individual) to put the mechanical "pieces" together before you can begin your repetitions. As your stroke changes, your touch may change a bit, too. You probably will be stroking the ball more solidly, so that it rolls a little farther with what feels like the same amount of stroke energy. And remember, your goal for touch is to develop the instinct to roll the ball 17 inches past the hole. You need to spend some time on the putting games as described in Chapter 14, along with your practice of mechanics.

Of course, I realize you may not have as much time as you'd like to devote to improving your putting. So I'm going to suggest three putting practice schedules, one of which should be right for you. They call for one, two, or three hours of practice per week.

Decide how much time you want to spend. You may be able to spend even more than three hours per week on your putting; if so, great! But whatever time you spend, make it quality time. It's better to work properly for one hour than to practice without feedback for three. To improve, you need to put in at least one hour's practice per week. That's just ten minutes a day, six days a week. Two hours per week means six twenty-minute sessions; three hours per week means six thirty-minutes sessions. Whichever you choose, try for regular practice sessions every day, rather than a single marathon session once a week.

For the first month devote your practice time to stroke mechanics; later you can work in practice on the putting games to develop your touch. For example, if you're going to improve your putter path by working in a putting track (Figure 21.1), in a ten-minute session carefully set up and execute thirty strokes (three per minute, or one every twenty seconds). Depending on how much time you spend per week, the results after one month will look like this:

SUCCESSFUL STROKES	1 HOUR/WEEK 10 MINUTES/DAY	2 HOURS/WEEK 20 MINUTES/DAY	3 HOURS/WEEK 30 MINUTES/DAY
Per day	30	60	90
Per week	180	360	540
First month	720	1440	2160

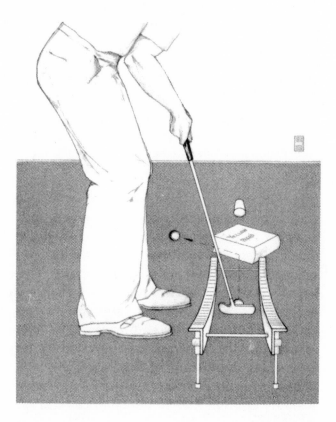

FIGURE 21.1:
Follow one of
the practice
regimens
suggested, and
watch your
putting results
steadily
improve.

After one month, start mixing in some work on touch by using the games in Chapter 14. When you practice touch, "shift gears" and focus your attention away from stroke mechanics and onto imparting the proper speed to the ball. Let your stroke mechanics go on "automatic control" during this phase of practice.

If you practice the games for touch once a week for the next two months, while staying on your stroke mechanics the other five days per week, at the end of three months you'll have completed the following:

SUCCESSFUL STROKES	1 HOUR/WEEK 10 MINUTES/DAY	2 HOURS/WEEK 20 MINUTES/DAY	3 HOURS/WEEK 30 MINUTES/DAY
First Month	720	1440	2160
Second Month	600	1200	1800
Third Month	600	1200	1800
Total Strokes	1920	3840	5760
Touch Session (one 30-minute session/week, eight weeks)	240 minutes	240 minutes	240 minutes

At the three-month mark, you will be well along in ingraining your new stroke path. In fact, if you're on the "accelerated" course (devoting three hours per week to your practice), you will have made significant progress toward your goal of 20,000 successful strokes, while adding several hours' worth of touch practice as well. On this schedule you will have already broken through any "regression period" and will definitely be seeing improvement in your putting results on the course. On the one-hour-per-week schedule, after three months you may not be much better, and you might even think you are a little worse. I cannot emphasize strongly enough that you *must* stick with it during this phase. Your day is coming!

After you have worked for three months, change the balance of your practice time and spend half on stroke mechanics (three sessions per week) and half (three sessions) on games for touch. Thus after six months, you'll have completed the following:

SUCCESSFUL STROKES	1 HOUR/WEEK 10 MINUTES/DAY	2 HOURS/WEEK 20 MINUTES/DAY	3 HOURS/WEEK 30 MINUTES/DAY
First 3 months	1920	3840	5760
Second 3 months	1080	2160	3240
Total Strokes	3000	6000	9000
Touch Practice			
First 3 months	240 minutes	240 minutes	240 minutes
Second 3 months	600 minutes	840 minutes	1080 minutes
Total	840 minutes (14 hours)	1080 minutes (18 hours)	1320 minutes (22 hours)

If you continue multiplying the practice sessions and successful strokes, you'll see that at the end of a year, under the one-hour-per-week regimen, you will be in the 6,000-stroke range (as well as having put in some solid work on your touch). You'll be an improved putter. It will take less than a year to reach the 10,000 stroke mark if you practice for two hours per week, and just over six months with three hours' practice per week. Whichever regimen you choose, continue it beyond 20,000 successful strokes. This will ensure that your new stroke mechanics are grooved and you couldn't go back to your faulty stroke even if you tried. Your muscles will believe that your "new" stroke is the only one you've ever known!

Of course, even after you've reached this point, continue practicing your stroke and touch, so you catch any errors that begin to creep in right at the start. Always practice your putting for a minimum of *one hour per week* to maintain a high-quality stroke. One hour is not very much time; it's probably less than you used to spend anyway, although now you'll be accomplishing much, much more.

GOOD LUCK, AND GOOD PUTTING

Now you understand my entire putting system. Put it to work at the pace that's right for you. No matter what putting ailments you've struggled with in the past, if you put your effort and patience into working with this system, you will become a vastly improved putter. You'll be able to take this newly developed ability with you to whatever course or tournament you play—and you will enjoy the great game of golf more than ever before.

So get to work with zest, my friend! You'll enjoy watching your ability go up, as more and more putts go down.